EUROPA
A Spiritual Biography

EUROPA
A Spiritual Biography

Richard Seddon

TEMPLE LODGE
London

Temple Lodge Publishing
51 Queen Caroline Street
London W6 9QL

Published by Temple Lodge 1995

A catalogue record for this book is available from the British Library

ISBN 0 904693 72 4

Cover by S. Gulbekian. Inset: The Archangel Joel, a Rumanian-Byzantine painting from the Monastery of Moldovita. © Raffael-Verlag, Switzerland. Reproduced with permission

Typeset by DP Photosetting, Aylesbury, Bucks
Printed and bound in Great Britain by Cromwell Press Limited, Broughton Gifford, Wiltshire

CONTENTS

Preface 7

Introduction 9

1 THE PREVIOUS SUN REGENCY OF MICHAEL—
CLASSICAL GREECE
Mid-sixth to third century BC 18

2 THE SATURN REGENCY OF ORIPHIEL—
THE ROMAN EMPIRE
Second century BC to mid-second century AD 26

3 THE VENUS REGENCY OF ANAEL—
THE AGE OF MIGRATIONS
Mid-second to fifth century 33

4 THE JUPITER REGENCY OF ZACHARIEL—
THE DAWN OF PERSONAL INTELLIGENCE
Sixth to mid-ninth century 42

5 THE MERCURY REGENCY OF RAPHAEL—
CHRISTENDOM (PERSONAL FEELING)
Mid-ninth to twelfth century 50

6 THE MARS REGENCY OF SAMAEL—
CORPORATE AND PERSONAL WILLING
Thirteenth to fifteenth century 60

7 THE MOON REGENCY OF GABRIEL—
PERSONAL EGOISM, NATIONAL EGOISM
Sixteenth century to 1879 72

8 THE PRESENT SUN REGENCY OF MICHAEL—
THE BATTLE FOR THE SPIRIT
From 1879 to the twenty-second century 93

CONCLUSION 110

REFERENCES 115

BIBLIOGRAPHY 123

PREFACE

This study is in no sense a survey of European history as researched by professional historians. It is, rather, an attempt to bring together into a single focus the essence of the published results of the spiritual research into history undertaken by Rudolf Steiner (1861–1925) so far as this relates to Europe, and to set it against a sketch of outer events. The description presupposes an understanding of the spiritual nature of man and of the universe, at least to the extent that this is given in his book *Occult Science, an Outline.*

As Britons we have lived for centuries in the splendid isolation of islanders, but our interests have been world-wide. Now we find ourselves called upon to regard ourselves as Europeans, but must consider whether this is an expansion of our nationhood or a contraction of our consciousness. A nation is clearly a reality, having its own territory, people, government, often language, way of life and much else—from a spiritual point of view, its common Folk Spirit. But is Europe also a spiritual reality, or merely a conglomeration of nations who happen to be located close to one another? What sort of being stands behind it? Are Britain and the Commonwealth of Independent States really part of it? In search of an answer to such questions we must look to history.

An overview such as this cannot enter into the spiritual depths of the events described. Here the references to Rudolf Steiner's own works are of great importance, enabling the serious student to find readily his full elaboration of particular points. Such references cannot be exhaustive, but provide at least a starting point for further study.

It is a pleasure to record here the very substantial help received from Terry Boardman, whose professional ability as a historian and critical mind have saved me from many pitfalls and added considerable substance to the whole, especially for the period of the present Michael age. Without his cooperation and encouragement the project would probably never have reached completion.

Richard Seddon
Advent 1994

INTRODUCTION

The Role of History

History is the result of all that human beings have done, in all its multifariousness and complexity. But it is illusory to think that all such deeds are caused by the immediately preceding events. Actions may arise—often in the darkness of unconsciousness—from the interaction of many influences, which in spiritual science (Anthroposophy) are understood to proceed from spiritual beings other than ourselves. These may be beings higher than humanity, Angels (who guide individuals), Archangels (who guide nations or similar groups), Archai (who guide the development of a cultural age) or yet higher beings. They may be the opposing powers in evolution known as Lucifer (the tempter, who would hold man back in pride at achievements based on the past, and draw him away from progressive evolution), or Ahriman (the father of lies, who denies the reality of spirit and would hold human beings in his power). They may lie in influences from the deceased. Or they may lie in tendencies within the individual himself, either conscious or unconscious, arising from his experiences and deeds in a previous life or in this one. The broader our insight into the working of such influences in the course of history, the better our context in which to assess the events of the present moment. For much of what comes to expression today has its roots in the past.

If we are to gain knowledge of mankind from a world aspect, we must observe history from the aspect of a spiritual science which moves between heaven and earth. We have to attain a living, sympathetic interest in events, a longing to go beyond ordinary history, and to seek out that history which must and can be read in the living spirit. There are times when what has real being and essence comes to the surface as a symptom, and if one can penetrate more deeply it can be judged with discernment from the phenomena. It is important to turn our attention to those decisive turning points when the life of the soul turns from one stage of development to the next, usually overlooked in the tangled skein of events.[1]

It is particularly important today to perceive in detail not only how the human being is a reflection of the supersensible world, but how historical events are also reflections of the supersensible. This is the only path by which we can find our way back again to the divine-spiritual world. Human history can only be considered in its true reality when one learns to know the individual actuating spiritual forms that stand behind it, just as one can only get to know nature when one knows in its true form what works and lives behind sense-perceptions.[2]

The Articulation of Time

Although the years roll by in a continuum which appears to be undifferentiated, they are in fact differentiated by the course of the vernal point of the sun, the nutation of the moon, and similar cosmic rhythms. We are in history especially concerned with the working of seven specific Archangels who, instead of governing a group of people, take precedence in turn to guide evolution for a period of some 300 to 400 years under the direction of the guiding Archon or Spirit of the Age. Dates defining such periods were given long ago by Trithemius of Sponheim (1487–1516), based on the astronomical fact that during a period of $354\frac{1}{3}$ years 'Saturn performs the same number of revolutions through the zodiac as the moon in a synodic year (12 months of $29\frac{1}{2}$ days = 354 days); each such revolution thus appears as a kind of month in the whole period. The Archangel period may thus be seen as an image of the transition from the eternal to the cyclical realms, and again from the cyclical to the transitory realm represented by the single period.'[3]

Rudolf Steiner knew of Trithemius' work, and referred to it in an early lecture. But when he came to the Torquay conference of 1924, he brought a notebook in which he had written different dates, the earlier ones increasingly approximated. In speaking he referred to the periods only in terms of centuries, and we may suppose that his research had shown him meanwhile that the activities of spiritual beings are not rigidly determined by the astronomical phenomena, but continue to work strongly while the next impulse begins. Indeed, for the last Michael age his notebook showed the period 550 to 200 BC, whereas he had earlier remarked in London that 'soon after the Mystery of Golgotha had taken place ... the direct influence of Michael had ended', and later he called the age 'four or five centuries'.[4]

The respective dates of commencement may be summarized as follows:

Archangel	*Planet*	*Trithemius*	*Steiner notebook*
Michael	Sun	1879	1879
Gabriel	Moon	1525	1510
Samael	Mars	1171	1190
Raphael	Mercury*	817	850
Zachariel	Jupiter	463	500
Anael	Venus*	109	150
Oriphiel	Saturn	246 BC	200 BC
Michael	Sun	599 BC	550 BC

*Steiner has pointed to a historical confusion between the names of the inner planets as interest shifted from the temporal to the spatial sequence. In spiritual science (as for the ancients) Venus is the name given to the planet nearer to the sun, Mercury that nearer to moon and earth. But depending on his audience, Steiner sometimes used the usual and opposite nomenclature. His sequence is the key.[5]

The Archai, the Hierarchy next above the Archangels, are also known specifically as Time Spirits or Spirits of Personality. Their work is concerned with the development of human consciousness over longer cultural epochs of 2160 years, one twelfth of the Platonic Cosmic Year of 25,920 years taken by the vernal point of the sun to traverse the zodiac. This indicates some independence between the two Hierarchies in that $7 \times 354\frac{1}{3}$ years = 2480 years, not 2160.

The consideration of events in each archangelic period in relation to their influences makes possible a more structured view of history than is otherwise possible. There are, of course, other rhythms of time which cannot be incorporated in the present study. It should be noted that the dates given after personal names *are not* the usual ones of birth and death, but indicate the years of influential creative work, either by the earliest and latest deeds significant for recorded history or by the ages of 25 and 65.

The Geography of Europe

The limits of the continent to north, west and south are sufficiently obvious, but many people are unaware how distant is the eastern limit accepted both politically and by spiritual science that is set by the Urals and the Caspian Sea. Indeed we have been so spellbound by the old USSR that what is often called Eastern Europe is physically in fact relatively central. The Carpathians, Alps and Pyrenees form a giant backbone from east to west, but this starts little less than half the way from the distant Urals. This backbone until recently restricted, but did not prevent, movement between north and south. Other ranges branch from it, from which great rivers drain in all directions towards the encircling seas. There is also a polarity between an extensive land mass (earth element) to the east and compressed peninsulas reaching into the great ocean (water element) to the west. Britain and Ireland have only been physically separated from the continent since about 6000 BC.

Looking etherically, we see two great arms of water reaching from west to east. To the north lie the English Channel, the North Sea (open to the north) and the Baltic Sea. This 'sea-dragon' and its tributaries actually carry everything that is spiritual in European humanity; had it still extended right to the Caspian as it once did—the Volga rises quite close to the Baltic—Russia would have been physically cut off from Asia, and would have developed prematurely all that is destined to arise there only in the future. To the south is the Mediterranean, extending up into the Black Sea, which has borne so much of Europe's earthly destiny in the past, and is in contrast totally enclosed.[6]

It is to be remembered that while the waters flow down to these seas, ever new, the eternal etheric streams—for example 'Old Father Thames'—flow upwards towards the mountains, counterbalancing the physical and bearing with them the early traders and settlers. Particularly of the Danube, flowing back from east to west through the heart of Central Europe, has this been true.

Europa

The term 'Europe' is first known to have been used in a geographical sense by Herodotus (484 BC). Previously, for example for Hesiod (800), Europa was a goddess, the name being interpreted variously as 'well-watered', 'broad face' or 'good impulse'. According to legend, Europa was carried off from Phoenicia (and thus arose as a Phoenix) by Zeus in the form of a white bull (in the age of the Bull). Zeus represents the impulse of the Jupiter Oracle of Atlantis, whose special task was directed to the nerves serving the outer senses and to the brain, the distinctive feature of European civilization compared with the Asian cultures which preceded it. Zeus took her to Crete, where she bore him three sons. The eldest was Minos, founder of the Minoan culture (2500–1400 BC)—the name is the same word as Manas, mind. The other sons were Radamanthys ('diviner with wand', suggesting the druidic element) and Sarpedon ('rejoices in wooden ark', suggesting the Hebraic/church stream)—together fundamental influences on the culture to come.

Minos' wife had a passion for another white bull, and gave birth to a monster, half human but with a bull's head, called the Minotaur, representing a primitive condition of mankind. She therefore ordered Daedalus to build a labyrinth beneath the palace to contain it. Daedalus had been taught by Pallas Athene, goddess of intellectual knowledge, had acquired the magic sword of thinking, and had discovered how to make wings of wax and feathers with which to fly—that is, he was the master of cosmic thinking, with which he made the labyrinth of the brain.

The Minotaur, duly installed, demanded regular tribute of seven youths and seven maidens, and Theseus volunteered. He had acquired his sword from the rock, like King Arthur; had destroyed a fierce and monstrous white sow, that is, had been initiated in the Mysteries; had invented wrestling; and had driven off Medusa. Now he acquired from Ariadne, his lover, a magic ball of thread given her by Daedalus, which enabled him to enter the labyrinth, overcome the Minotaur, and also find his way out again.[7]

In this picture the Greek Mysteries portrayed what they foresaw as the destiny of Europe.

The Soul of Europe

The legend of Zeus means that Europeans were from the start influenced by the forces of Jupiter, which work through the sensory nerves. The predominance of one or several senses in the different localities gave rise to differences in form, determined national tendencies, and resulted in different tasks. The Greeks, for example, originally perceived the spiritual clairvoyantly while they saw the physical, and hence became the basic people for all sculpture and external form-giving. These distinctions were later distorted by force of arms or political considerations.

Europeans have thus the task to tread the path to the spirit through the senses. Modern thinking is strongly coloured by the sense of smell at the root of the nose, but directed inwards to the processes of life-ether; mathematics is based on the senses of movement and balance, and the concepts of science are based primarily on the sense of touch (weight and measure). All the senses are in fact seeds for the development of higher faculties.[8]

Into the peoples determined by the physical senses work the Folk Spirits, Archangels who are active in the ground forces, vegetation, water and climate of a region, and in the etheric bodies and specially the temperaments of the people living there, giving rise to the particular nature of the Folk. Folk Spirits share in the moral and artistic ideals of a people, their mythological wisdom, religions and sciences, aiming to stir lethargy into inner activity.[9]

All Folk Spirits are Christian, though on a different plane from man, having regarded Christ as their teacher since they passed through the human stage on Old Sun. Even during the First World War the Folk Souls of Europe lived together harmoniously in a kind of choir—it is the individuals of a nation who may or may not be Christian. The various nationalities will, however, have to work together, if they are to become the soul of Europe.[10]

Prehistory

As far back as Hyperborean times, when evolution had not condensed further than warmth and air, a highly spiritual culture existed in the region of Greenland, of which traces were later carried into the Northern Mysteries. After Lemuria, the races were differentiated in early Atlantis; the white race was under the guidance of the Jupiter Oracle situated in the north Atlantic.

As the end of Atlantis approached, the most advanced human beings, namely, those with some primitive ability to have thoughts (but consequently the least clairvoyant), were led by Manu across Europe to a centre near the Gobi Desert, from which the cultures of India, Persia and Egypt were later nurtured.[11] The remarkable cave art of France and Spain, revealing a great love of animals, derives from this time. So does the Basque language, and probably Finnish and Georgian. Those from the Jupiter Oracle dropped off *en route* to form a great centre in northern Germany, in the region of Paderborn/Detmold. There is also considerable evidence around the Danube and Dniepr of a matriarchal society reaching back to that time, centred on the White Lady, the moon goddess, with a striking absence of horses, images of warfare, or male domination.

Then in the fifth millennium BC, in complete contrast, peoples of the Indo-European culture spread back westwards. As these peoples settled by the sea, in the mountains, or on the plains, both their physical bodies and their speech were shaped further from outside by the various nature spirits under the guidance of the archangelic Folk Spirits—whereas in Asia they had been shaped more by forces within their own etheric bodies.[12]

It was to a branch of the Hibernian Mysteries that reached eastwards from Ireland as far as Hungary that about 3000 BC, at the beginning of the sentient soul age, Gilgamesh travelled from Chaldea. Before the middle of the following millennium there is evidence that initiates from Chaldea had brought a fresh impulse as far west as Ireland, developing the megalithic culture. This took the form of centres of initiation, religion and scientific observation of the rhythms of time expressed in the movements of the starry heavens. This was in many ways the polar opposite of the contemporary Egyptian culture, which looked inwards and to the measurement of space.

The second millennium BC saw the Bronze Age in Europe, and the movement of the future Greeks from the Caspian to the eastern Mediterranean, where city states were being established by 1200 BC.[13]

1
THE PREVIOUS SUN REGENCY OF MICHAEL—CLASSICAL GREECE

Mid-sixth to third century BC

Michael and the Sun Quality

Michael ('who is like God'?) has been long renowned as the conqueror of the dragon, the lower forces that rise up in man. He does not kill the dragon, but subdues it to his powerful will. His cosmic sword is the meteor shower of autumn, which has its counterpart in the iron within our blood. Michael is also the Ruler of the Cosmic Intelligence—what the Hierarchies do, how they relate to one another—for the benefit of humanity. In spring, his forces live in all our expressions of will, in all that comes to movement in us. His rulership is always characterized by the growth of cosmopolitanism. During this period he was experienced during sleep, and was known to the Hebrews as the countenance of Jehovah.[14]

The sun is pre-eminently a colony of the Second Hierarchy, and delimits the activity of the Spirits of Form. The sphere bounded by the sun is the highest region of Soul-land, known as Soul Life, a realm of eternal growth and development. Here the soul is freed after death from any idea that material objects have any reality greater than, for example, a rainbow. This is expressed in the soul mood of empiricism, which simply accepts phenomena without any theorizing.[15]

The sun is the source not only of light but of life and love. The whole human being is an expression of the sun forces, especially the blood circulation centred in the heart. The sun forms the basis for our ordinary everyday consciousness, and illumines all intellectual life. The inner organ for perception of the Sun Mysteries is the period of the prime of life, between the ages of 21 and 42.[16]

The End of the Mysteries

A new stage in the gradual development of human consciousness had already begun a couple of centuries before Michael took up his rulership, namely, the cultural age that was to develop the mind soul (later the intellectual soul), starting in 747 BC and lasting until AD 1413. That is the part of the soul which gradually becomes interwoven with independent thoughts transcending immediate sense experience. It had been heralded in Greece by the writings of Homer (850), the first Olympiad (776), and the introduction of coinage (700).

Civilization was at that time still guided from the Mysteries, where pupils were led to give birth in consciousness to the god spellbound within them, their higher ego. The Greek Mysteries were a continuation of those inspired in Persia by Zarathustra long before, despite the outer conflicts culminating in the battles of Marathon (490) and Salamis (480). It was to Persia that such initiates as Pythagoras (553–515) went in search of wisdom. Ahura Mazdao, the spirituality behind the sun's forces, became Apollo, who with his muses made the earth resound with the harmonies of the spheres. Apollo was an Angel being ensouled by Christ prior to His descent from sun to earth. At Delphi Apollo shot his arrows against the Python writhing in the vapours mounting from the abyss, as Michael fought the dragon, and it was from him that guidance for social and political life was sought.[17]

The Mysteries of Ephesus, with its temple of Artemis

(550), were of profound significance. The Word, the Logos, was seen as the primal source of creation of the world, of mankind, and of the individual—as St John later expressed it. The way in which a word became speech was compared with the process of incarnation. The Mysteries of Eleusis portrayed in Demeter the culture of Atlantis, of which the Greek age was a recapitulation. As representative of the primal laws of nature, Demeter was also the source of moral law. Her daughter Persephone represented the ancient clairvoyance, whose destiny it was to dwell for a time in the darkness of the subconscious, as well as the soul itself as it passes through life and death.[18]

There were many other mystery centres in Europe, and not only in Greece. It was said at Delphi that when in winter the sun moved south Apollo travelled north; indeed, Diodorus (60–21) said that Apollo was born in the north, and he described a round temple like Stonehenge. The peoples of 'barbarian' Europe—mainly Celts, with as yet undifferentiated Germanic-Slav tribes to the north-east—had their Mysteries, even though their culture was that of the Iron Age. The Hibernian Mysteries from Atlantis were still active in Ireland, centred on the Boyne; the Arthurian Mysteries at Tintagel were open to the spiritual cosmos and the life between death and rebirth; there were the Mysteries of the Black Madonna at Chartres; the Northern Mysteries at the Externsteine near Paderborn; the Mysteries of Scythianos on the White Sea; the Mysteries of the Golden Fleece at Colchis, north of the Black Sea; and others. The Scandinavian Mysteries spoke in tragic tones of the Twilight of the Gods, and this came to archetypal physical expression in the destruction of Ephesus by arson in 356 BC. Prior to that, the world was regarded as a kind of earthly spiritland, and people were in constant soul-union with the gods.[19]

Changes in Consciousness

Thinking in ancient Greece was so different from ours that it is difficult to find a way to understand it. The early Greek gave himself over to outer impressions, and perceived with them the many elemental beings at work. The Angels—the gods of mythology—inhabited his body, shared his perceptions and, from their awareness of the deeds of the spiritual beings concerned, brought about a conceptual content which shone out from all the details in imaginations full of life. (Socrates later called this Angel his 'daimon'.) The individual needed to make no effort, and did not yet feel himself as an independent person. This thought content arose in space when the sun rose and disappeared when it set, hence it was regarded as an offspring of the sun's life. Therefore people spoke of the Cosmic Intelligence, the deeds and interrelationships of the spiritual Hierarchies, as being under the rulership of Michael, ruler of the sun. Beyond the blue sky they divined the existence of the thought-world of the gods. But cosmic events were then experienced only in dim astral vision, hence they spoke only vaguely of destiny or earthly fate.[20]

Then waking consciousness began to change. Memory, which had hitherto depended on rhythm to carry long recitals such as the work of Homer, began to take on the pictorial form it has today. In place of the Furies depicted in early drama when an immoral deed was performed, Euripedes (445) could depict the emergence of conscience. Thinking also changed. A sort of uniform world intelligence (nous) was now felt to fill the world objectively, arranging the phenomena outside man; and the etheric body was experienced as continuous with this surrounding elemental world. (This led to monotheism.) But thinking brought the etheric body into movement, refreshing the soul with life and stirring it to action. It was felt that to correspond with reality, thoughts must grow from a seed of wonder at the world, develop in a mood of reverence, be brought into wisdom-filled harmony with the world, and be received in an attitude of surrender to world reality.[21]

Gradually thought-pictures were felt to rise into consciousness from within the etheric body, somewhat as we experience a memory but out of the temperament. That is why Thales (600) found the origin of the world in water, Anaximenes (600) in air, and Heraclitus (500) in fire. For the same reason Hippocrates (460–429) laid the foundations of medicine on the basis of these four elements, held together by man's soul and spirit; the human being was for him a living work of art, perceptible in both a sensible and a supersensible manner. Whereas human deeds had hitherto been seen as inspired by the gods, Herodotus (488–425) now described history in an outward manner.

This was already a mainly urban culture, linked by sea with the coasts of Italy, the eastern Mediterranean and the Black Sea. The Greek male felt himself far less as an individual than as a member of his city-state, in whose collective decisions he participated on a democratic footing. It was, however, a culture based on the citizen's luciferic contempt for work—even for artistic work—and dependent on the subservience of women and the use of slaves (many of them well-educated people captured in battle). In other words, the individual ego of others was not yet recognized.[22]

The glory of Greek culture lay largely in its incomparable art. The imagination of artists was still alive with myths of the gods, which had been created within the Mysteries as garments for wisdom concerning processes of soul and spirit, and with legends such as those of Homer. The widespread art of tragedy (Euripedes, Sophocles, *c.* 450) enacted ritual secrets of the inner world of darkness and unconsciousness, elevated by poetry and music, which had a cathartic effect on the listeners. The outward gaze was enlivened and shaped by a most sensitive architecture, and by sculptures of grace, controlled energy and natural dignity, portraying man in the prime of life. Through this high development of phantasy, luciferic powers sought to achieve what they had failed to achieve during Atlantis, namely, to draw human beings away into their own realm of premature perfection and thus prevent further evolution. And it was the philosophers, whose thoughts intermingled with those of the poets, who were to prevent this from happening. The soul-atmosphere became filled, however, with the jealousy of the adverse powers at the continuing influence of the Mysteries.[23]

The Fourth Century BC

The great philosophy of Plato (385–347) embodied an echo of mystery wisdom. His teacher Cratylus had been a pupil of Heraclitus, and Plato's ideas are full of his world-creative principles. He felt his heart and limbs as still united with the surrounding spiritual world, but his head as isolated in the cave of the sense-world. His famous image of thoughts as shadows cast by reality on the cave wall established the idea as a dead shadow of the spirit. He portrayed Socrates (445–400) as if by activating thinking he enabled the mind of the universe to speak out of his very depths of soul. Plato thus regarded the capacity of the human soul to 'know itself' as belonging to eternity. Such thoughts were cultivated not only in the Platonic Academy (385) but for the next 2000 years.[24]

After the war between Athens and Sparta (477–379) a fresh impulse came from Aristotle (367–321), who had never been connected with the Mysteries. He used thinking as an instrument to delve into the objects of nature and to find the ideas that are actually part of them, which he still perceived alongside the sense-perceptions. This is the mood of empiricism, and a step towards the object-consciousness of today. Directing this mood to the soul itself, he distinguished the spiritual soul from the bodily soul, which has plantlike, sentient, desiring and willing parts. The spiritual soul he saw as a drop of the cosmic spirit separated out by the body, which afterwards lived on immortally. His research into the laws inherent in thinking itself led him to develop logic, which can no more be doubted than any other percept. These ideas stir the soul into activity, and through his Peripatetic School also worked into later ages.[25]

The campaigns of Alexander (334–321) were a late attempt to fructify with the new dynamic Greek impulse the ancient wisdom of the East. First was the conquest of Egypt, and the founding of Alexandria as a cosmopolitan centre of learning. Then was the conquest of Persia, even marrying into its ruling class. And finally was the approach to India, the fount of the post-Atlantean epoch. This was not destined to succeed, and after his death his empire fell apart.

The period of Decline

During the third century, consciousness of the spiritual world was generally lost and the Cosmic Word was no longer experienced. But awareness of the elemental world continued, and the ego still felt itself living not in the body but within the world of blossoming flowers, of thunder and rain. Plato and Aristotle were understood less and less; only abstract ideas and words remained.[26] Euclid published his geometry (323), Archimedes (260–212) developed the screw, lever and principle of flotation, and Eratosthenes made a good estimate of the earth's size and propounded that it moved round the sun (242). But philosophy itself became barren and negative: the Stoic ideal of man was the sage devoid of vice; the Epicurean ideal was to be without pain or discomfort. The myth of Orpheus had once told of the path of the initiate down to Hades, to free from its clutches Eurydice, the soul. Now it was known that this path could no longer be taken. Hence there emerged a fear of death: better a beggar on earth than a king in the realm of shades. We recognize the dawn of a new culture but, at the same time, the beginning of a severe world-historical illness.[27]

Thereafter Greece was of no great significance, as the Greeks themselves sensed. In 14 BC they came under Roman control. To understand this, we must consider the Greek Folk Spirit. Though active from the start, this being only completed his development after the great struggles with Persia. He then rose comparatively quickly, as Greek culture spread, to a leading position as Spirit of the Age throughout the eastern Mediterranean coastal area, and thus from Archangel to Archon. He could have ascended further to the realm of Spirits of Form, to work on through the ages as did the Spirit of the Egyptian Age. But almost at the moment that the Christ-impulse came to earth he renounced this for the present, and became instead the Spirit of Exoteric Christianity—its missionary impulse. Thus the Greeks lost their Folk Spirit and, particularly because of their contempt for work, the Greek culture went under. But their language was preserved by the Eastern Church.

During the first third of the age of the mind soul, the soul is thus freed from its vision with the spiritual world and feels itself withdrawn into a separate human totality. The spirit of Greek culture must rise again, but from within each person—and it will arise. Then the path to the Mysteries will be found once more, and in like manner the path to Christ also.[28]

2
THE SATURN REGENCY OF ORIPHIEL— THE ROMAN EMPIRE

Second century BC to mid-second century AD

Oriphiel and the Saturn Forces

Oriphiel is otherwise known only as the leader of those planetary intelligences who since the ninth century AD began to emancipate themselves from the rule of Michael.*[29]

The forces of Saturn reach back to the earliest incarnation of the earth, a condition of courage and fiery will, into which the primal germs of the twelve senses were laid. These forces express the Cosmic Word as such, out of which everything was created. This Cosmic Word, the innermost and deepest Cosmic 'I', resounds in primordial spirit-inwardness. The Saturn Mysteries can thus unveil the very depths of the cosmos.[30]

As the outermost of the traditional planets, Saturn forms a boundary to the solar system. So its work in humanity is both isolating and individualizing, yet must adapt to what is beyond. Its gesture is blue, which tends to form a periphery. Saturn works through the senses lying on the surface of the body, especially the eye. It creates these senses as the physical basis for the lower ego, making man into a being of earth. In the lower organism it works in the spleen,

* Uriel ('God is my light'), the Archangel of midsummer, when the earth breathes furthest out to cosmic distances, is also one of the seven Archangels of Time. This is probably a different aspect of the being here named Oriphiel.

again forming a sieve through which the rhythms of the foodstuffs are modified and outer influences thus excluded from our inner being.[31]

Saturn also preserves the Cosmic Memory, of which it speaks with warmth and devotion; and it is the source of human memory, without which there can be no ego-consciousness. It is the pledge of moral freedom, being the root of the moral forces in the universe, which shape human karma.[32] It works right into the muscles and bones, into what we do, even the impulses to lie down or stand upright. But it can cause fixation in the physical body.[33]

Saturn forms the third region of Spirit-land, a sphere containing the archetypes of the soul world (desires, wishes, feelings), where after death our service to the community bears fruit. It also places into us our instincts. The soul mood of Saturn is gnosis, which seeks to know reality through the deepest sources within the soul, especially in spiritual matters. It gives impartial knowledge of ourself in relation to the progress of civilization. An organ for the perception of Saturn forces is life between ages 56 and 63.[34]

Roman Administration

Rome, founded in 753, had replaced its legendary kingship by a republic as early as 510 and started to codify its laws in 450, which thus received a strong moral impulse from the thinking of the Angels still experienced at that time.

In the new age, thinking was still directly viewed rather than 'thought', but was stimulated from outside through the senses and experienced in the sentient body, the centre of outer human activity. It was therefore suited to practical problems and outer organization, but not to spiritual life. So Rome produced no great original thinkers; nor did the arts go far beyond copying the Greeks, for phantasy was lacking. We can well understand Roman thinking today.[35]

Everything else was based on the Latin language or, rather, the Spirit of Latin behind it. This was itself logical and, when fanned to flame by the emotions that always stood behind Roman life, produced great orators and leaders. Education then consisted indeed in the pursuit of grammar, rhetoric and dialectics, which took on a new life.[36]

The mysteries surviving in Rome were a decadent form of the Egyptian Mysteries of space, measure and weight. But the grand scale of the wisdom and ritual of Egypt was missing in this prosaic age. Rome's strength lay in applying the Egyptian concept of hierarchy—which once expressed grades of spiritual development—to the army, the regional administration and, later, to the Church.

After the intermittent Punic wars against Egypt (260–149), Greece and Asia Minor were subdued, and by 31 BC Spain, Gaul and Britain had been added. By AD 100 the empire reached from Mesopotamia to Scotland (though not north of the Danube) and 1600 km of frontiers such as Hadrian's wall were being defended. The Roman Folk Spirit completed its incarnation during these conflicts, which tempered the Roman character, and it then rose as Spirit of the Age to the rank of Archon.[37]

The ahrimanic powers reckoned on a world empire in which all religious, artistic and other activities would be strictly controlled centrally in a great state machine that excluded all individuality. Roman history is fundamentally a struggle against this, by means of the moral justice expressed in legal ideals of human rights, as well as political and military ideals. The law ensured liberty for male citizens, though women were viewed as chattels. Property law aimed at harmony between owner and citizen, and extended to the right of disposal after death—an echo of Egyptian mummification.[38]

People at this time needed to be firmly anchored in the organism, otherwise they would only have felt themselves as an outer husk for the ego that they would only have experienced in sleep. The concept of man was therefore defined in a purely sense-bound manner between birth and death. As foundation for the personality, personal memory was developed. The ego was thus placed among other egos with definite rights, and the human being became an earth being standing upright on his own feet, into which the 'I' could fully descend. This was what the Romans had to accomplish in order to give importance to the 'I'. But later the extension of rights to all males who served the empire brought decline into a culture in which the state was regarded as superior to the single personality.[39]

The Celts

The Celtic peoples, who had spread across Europe north of the Danube to form the proto-European culture, were energetic, alert and cultured, interested in everything to do with man except his relation to the cosmos. They still had living intercourse with the elemental world, and spoke of nature spirits, water and earth genii. Their sensitivity is evident in the exquisite workmanship of their decorative art, for example in the Gundestrup cauldron (AD 200). They had a strong community life based on aristocracy, and were fine horsemen and fierce warriors, inclined to radical ideas.[40]

The Celts in Gaul, who had sacked Rome in 300 BC and overrun northern Italy (350–264), annihilated in 105 BC a Roman army of 80,000. The conquest of Gaul by Caesar (55) and his subsequent conquest of Britain was therefore a major achievement. In the next centuries the Celts were decimated and driven to the western promontories, though largely undisturbed in Germany. Their unfinished civilization is again explicable only by reference to their Folk Spirit, which had remained unaffected by the Greek and

Roman Spirits of the Age. With the descent of Christ this Celtic Folk Spirit withdrew to become the Spirit of Esoteric Christianity, renouncing further ascent.

Between the second century before and the second century after the Mystery of Golgotha the Germanic tribes were already moving into Europe from Asia, possibly from the Tarim basin, from which the cultures of India, Persia and Egypt were initiated.[41]

Forces of Death and Resurrection

The time came when an emperor—Augustus (BC 16–AD 14)—demanded to be initiated, like a Pharaoh, though he made no wrong occult use of it. He wanted to suppress all that the mind soul brought, and to allow only the sentient soul to come to expression by reviving all the significant and powerful rituals of the previous age. But as the sanctity of the Mysteries became successively violated by later emperors, and its secrets were extracted by force, the empire was plunged into moral darkness. In Caligula (AD 37–42) power to distinguish right from wrong no longer existed, and in Nero (61–68) all the devilish things belonging to an unworthy initiate are to be found—the old world was indeed going up in flames.[42]

Into this saturnine and indeed saturnalian situation came, not from Oriphiel but from cosmic depths, the impulse and sacrifice of Christ Jesus. Christ descended from the sun-sphere into the special human being Jesus, passed through the Mystery of Golgotha and rose again. This, the greatest of all Mysteries, is far beyond the scope of this study to characterize. To the lowest point of Earth evolution—though 333 years before the midpoint of the post-Atlantean epoch—it brought the forces of redemption not for the spirit (which did not need it) but for the souls of people. From the depths of Cosmic Egohood, Christ brought the spark of the real 'I', which was to catch fire within the freedom of every earthly individual in due time. Little of the full depth of this event has yet been grasped by human consciousness.[43]

The Gnostics realized that the highest wisdom was indeed to understand the Christ event, and attempted to do so through that knowing which survived from the Greek Mysteries. They were enabled to kindle a new inner light, and knew Christ both as the Logos and as the Sun Being who through His descent enabled the Hierarchies to work in a new way. They spoke, like St Paul, of body, soul and spirit (1 Corinthians 15:44), but they supposed Christ to be supersensible only, and did not grasp His actual relationship to Jesus.[44]

The Roman Senate was, however, intent on suppressing all knowledge of the spirit, and indeed of everything deriving from the Mysteries, especially the Jewish secret teaching. Gnostic views were not disproved, but simply eradicated in favour of a simplistic view of the Roman gods. Emperors from Tiberius (6–37) onwards perceived through their forced initiation the far-reaching significance of Christ, and wished to accept Him as a god alongside other Roman deities, but they were vigorously frustrated by the Senate. Most Romans, being dominated by the forces of old age, were unable to receive the quite new forces of Christianity.[45]

To ensure that all power lay in Roman hands, all other mystery centres and mystery wisdom were ruthlessly exterminated. For example, the Celtic college of Alesia on the Côte d'Or with 10,000 students was forcibly suppressed; and in Britain most of the druids were driven to Angelsey and slaughtered in AD 59. Here spoke Ahriman. Nevertheless something of spiritual knowledge was carried over, hidden in symbols understood only by very few.

The later emperors were not satisfied to be initiates—they insisted on being worshipped as gods. Here spoke Lucifer. Romans did not at that time believe in otherworldly gods but they did believe in human beings becoming divine and treated them accordingly, not out of obsequiousness but out of confidence. Tolerance of other religions was professed, so long as the divinity of the emperor was recognized. But to do this was impossible for Jews or Christians—hence the sack of Jerusalem (70), the dispersal (135) and the persecution of Christian martyrs. Nevertheless Christianity did survive in the catacombs of Rome.[46]

Meanwhile the tone of Christ's voice, the Cosmic Word itself, passed on by word of mouth from the original disciples, was losing its intimate power. In its place a gospel had in fact existed from AD 70. The reality of the Last Supper was transformed into the symbol of the Mass, the ritual of which incorporated much from the Egyptian and Eleusinian Mysteries. Later the Madonna (Isis) cult, the bishop's staff (sceptre of Osiris), the monstrance (sun and moon cult) and much else were added.[47]

From a deeper point of view it was a historical necessity that Europe should be separated off from the spiritual world by Rome, in order that each individual might out of his own freedom regain in due time a new relationship to the spirit from within himself. Ideas of law and justice which arose later point back to the justice of Rome, the Roman sense of rights. Nevertheless according to Christ this is, at its roots, anti-Christian. For He said: I tell you, not to oppose evil; love your enemies, and pray for those who persecute you (Matthew 5:39–42).[48]

3
THE VENUS REGENCY OF ANAEL—THE AGE OF MIGRATIONS
Mid-second to fifth century

The Nature of Venus

The name Anael ('God is merciful') is not used by Steiner in other contexts.

Venus speaks directly to the heart of beauty and love—for it is the mediator of cosmic love (or wrath, if hatred is present). Such love is born of love for the deed itself, and reaches as far as self-sacrifice. It comes from the realm known as Active Soul Force, which takes pleasure in action that is not egotistical. It delimits the sphere of the Spirits of Personality. It is concerned with the progress expressed in discoveries.[49]

Venus works most strongly between the ages of 14 and 21, when the forces of art draw into the adolescent who is karmically predisposed to them. It fills the sentient soul with feelings for what is perceived, and consequently also with ideals and religious impulses. It gives rise to the mood of mysticism, in which the soul becomes quiet and seeks inwardly for divine light.[50]

Spiritual Venus (see p. 11) also leads the incarnating soul down to its people, where it takes hold of the fluid system, especially the kidneys. Its quality manifests through the warm glow of copper, and it underlies the ten-petal lotus flower, which gives knowledge of among other things the realm of the deceased.[51]

This period is of special importance to anthroposophers,

many of whom then first came to know the earthly being of Christ Jesus. Those who knew him as Sun Being could hardly believe it, while others received Christianity through an intellect still permeated with feelings.[52]

Roman Christianity

Only at the end of the second century were the Apostles able to inspire the Church Fathers from their life after death. In a mighty poem, and in paintings and shrines, were expressed the descent of Christ into the man Jesus, and the development from youth to maturity of the scholar through the cult of the Virgin (but these were later vigorously exterminated by the Church). Non-Roman Christians in Britain were mentioned by Tertullian in AD 200. Elsewhere many Christians suffered martyrdom, especially in the time of Diocletian (303–05).[53]

Mithraism, the religion of the legions, spoke of Mithras as sun-god, whose task was to master the bull, the elemental planetary forces in the lower organism. Origen (225–54) tried to Christianize this, but Mithraism could not grasp the Incarnation. He also tried to prove that Christianity was compatible with Greek thought, and introduced the concept of destiny arising from a past incarnation—for which he was tortured. Plotinus (230–69) strove to reach philosophically beyond thinking, but found only a luciferic union of thought with the All One. His adherents formed the school of Neoplatonism.[54]

There was an important doctrinal dispute. Arius (275–325) experienced divinity as a mystical feeling *within* the soul, which, he maintained, must be developed in the way shown by Christ, the Son of God. He felt 'Not I, but Christ in me'. But Athanasius (315–61) thought of Christ as Himself truly God, enthroned in otherworldliness *outside* and above man, i.e. in Neoplatonic abstraction. Although one soul at the Council of Nicea (325) argued for a middle way, the Council decided in favour of Athanasius; and even emperors who believed Arius imposed Athanasianism as more supportive of the state.[55]

Constantine (306–37) shrank both from initiation and from carrying conflict with Christians into the Mysteries. In 312 he united the eastern and western empires under Rome, and perceiving that half the citizens in the East were Christians, he established tolerance in 313. Believing a prophecy of the fall of Rome (which Christians, interpreting it religiously, denied), he founded Constantinople near Troy (326–30), and in the statue of Apollo, moved from Rome, he had implanted pieces of the Cross and the Crown of Thorns—for he needed to express his intellectual understanding of Christianity in outer processes. On his deathbed he was finally baptized—by an Arian priest. Christianity was then imposed throughout the empire, but for political ends, as a belief, like a garment on the etheric body, instead of as a conviction of the mind.[56]

Everything thus became abstract, the Pope became a temporal prince, dioceses were defined by existing regions, and some bishops even became magistrates. Roman culture, based on slavery, was already remote from the thinking and feeling of the masses of people. In this way the Roman Spirit of the Age combined with the Spirit of Exoteric Christianity. But in all this the influence of Oriphiel was still active. In 354 Christmas was moved from Epiphany (6 January) to the Roman festival of the sun-god Mithras (25 December): from the incarnation of Christ to the birth of the Jesus-child.[57]

Julian the Apostate (361–63), who was properly initiated in the Mysteries of Eleusis, sought to restore the ancient gods, and then to find the transition to Manichaean Christianity, but he was assassinated by a Roman Christian. Thereafter the Eastern and Western Churches developed apart. Roman ideas were now based simply on factual

Gospel narrative and dogmatic abstractions in the dying Latin language. Western Christianity thus received a form that was spiritually darkened, through which Ahriman might well have gained control.

In contrast, Pelagius from the Celtic Church in Ireland was in Rome by 394. Since both the birth of Jesus and the Mystery of Golgotha had been perceived in the West clairvoyantly, transition from the Hybernian and Arthurian Mysteries to Christianity had been a natural and independent development without conflict. Pelagius preached free will, the rejection of predestination, and direct communion between the individual and Christ without priestly mediation, based on the text 'You shall know the truth, and the truth shall set you free'. If this had been taken up, many souls would inevitably have found union with the spiritual world. But it undermined any need for the Roman hierarchy, who claimed to be the unique dispensers of grace; so he was anathematized as a heretic. Germanus was sent to Britain (425, 446) not to convert more pagans but to eliminate Pelagianism among the converted. When Patrick reached Ireland in 432, he found a Celtic Church already active there.[59]

In the Spiritual World

The year 333 was the centre of the whole post-Atlantean epoch, and during this fourth century mighty changes surged beneath the level of human consciousness. The Spirits of Form (Exusiai), who on the sun had once breathed into man the living soul, and had hitherto stood behind the Angels as they shaped their pictorial thoughts within human beings, were withdrawing. Their cosmic task was instead taken over by the Archai (Spirits of Personality) who relate to the sphere of Venus. Now the Cosmic Intelligence ruled by Michael began to descend into human personalities, human hearts. Something which came from Christ Himself instilled into people the urge to respond with thoughts from out of their own being. We are no longer dealing with the perception of thoughts but with their production at first in the sentient soul, though they were not yet entirely the person's own activity. This enabled fresh elemental spirits from other worlds to work in the blood, bringing new moral impulses that will gradually help people to become individual personalities but also opening more opportunities to choose evil rather than good. The conception of God as All-Wise gave way to the conception of the Almighty.[60]

Augustine (380–430) had at first received the great thoughts of the oriental Christian teacher Manes (242), which in mighty images grasped both wisdom and goodness as within the light, that is to say, spiritual qualities within the physical. But Neoplatonism and the Church had no organ to understand this, so when his thoughts came under the Archai he could only fall back on tradition—he then saw baptism for example as important not for its purifying effect on souls but because there was an institution that baptized.

It was in this fourth century that Manes gathered round him in the spiritual world the personalities in whom Zarathustra (Nazarathos, the bearer of Christ), Scythianos and Buddha were living, the result of whose deliberations was the future European Mysteries of the Rose Cross.[61]

Gothic Christianity

The Goths, who occupied a wide area around Poland, Romania and southern Russia, now began to stir. Through them the Northern Mysteries, which spoke of both Lucifer and Ahriman (Loki and blind Hoeder), enter recorded history. They were courageous, practical people, with a strong feeling for nature and a premature longing for the ego, even in pre-Christian times. Their justice was originally simple: might is right. But they extolled the hero even when he failed, if he stood firm in rectitude of spirit and soul.[62] At the time of Christ they still had an extremely vigorous spiritual life, and participated in the work of Angels and Archangels (Aesir) as—up to the tenth century—they woke the 'I' out of the group soul. They still worshipped ancestral forces, alongside the mineral and fluid forces that rose from the blood as dreamlike clairvoyant pictures in the soul, which their priests then interpreted.[63]

So when those who had settled by the Black Sea before 200 came across Christianity, they felt Christ too as dwelling within the soul, a Man above all others, both spiritual and temporal Sovereign, and they had a natural affinity to Arianism. They took Christianity to heart with youthful energy, not as a belief but as a message of love for one another. Significantly, the Gospel was translated into Gothic by Ulfilas some 32 years before the Latin Vulgate of Jerome, and through it the Goths were eventually to change the whole future of Christianity in Europe.[64]

In 360 the Huns drove the Ostrogoths west into the land of the Visigoths. The Goths were at that time inspired by three Archangel beings—Wotan, Vili and Ve—who could direct peoples across the earth. As if in a dream, vast migrations took place. The Germanic peoples formed a kind of fountainhead for the rest of Europe. And through the effects of Arian Christianity on their feelings, forces of love and sacrifice started to unfold in their sentient souls. One may say that the Spirit of the Earth Himself was now working through their bloodstream, preparing peoples as His future vehicles. For it was not the ideas of Christianity nor its new morality which spread across Europe so mysteriously from east to west, but Christ Himself who as Spirit Self moved from soul to soul, from heart to heart. It is as though the ahrimanic mechanization of the empire which threatened to destroy Roman Christianity was being purged by the message of love.[65]

Wotan, bearing sun forces as spirit and life in thinking, also developed life forces in the Visigoths that gave them courage and presence of mind. About 380 he led them down into Greece, where for a generation they intermarried and moulded peasant life to the northern Arian festivals. Then after plundering Athens they moved up the Balkans and down into Italy, overrunning Rome in 410 despite the recall of troops from as far away as Britain. After two further generations of assimilation, nothing was left in Italy of the original Etruscan and Latin blood; without this, the power to develop ego-consciousness might have been lost.[66]

Then they moved on again through southern France to Spain (480). Here they settled, and the dreamy awareness of ancestral gods, led by Christ—a consolation while migrating—was replaced by an attachment to locality-gods of forest, mountain, streams. They used the cultured inhabitants as slaves, which enhanced their own consciousness. But the priests now had to interpret signs of nature, and this made them susceptible also to the symbolism and cult of Athanasian Rome. Gothic power was then soon broken, and they merged into the Spanish grandees of later centuries. Because of this impulse of Wotan in thinking, the whole of southern Europe remained under the domination of the priestly element.[67]

Germanic raiders had settled in south-east England since 170, and Germani in the Roman army probably remained here. After the Romans left there was a brief resurgence of Celtic shrines (Lydney 367) and of reverence for the elemental world; and a Celtic kingdom flourished under Coel Hen (Old King Cole, *c.* 420). Then around 450, Angles, Saxons and Jutes under the inspiration of Ve ('kind feeling') arrived in strength, though in Britain the greatest part of original blood remained. The settlers came from the north German coast where for 3000 years Nerthus/Erda/Earth, one of the older generation of Nordic gods, had regulated the process of birth. Although the cosmic aspect had been lost, this had prepared them to understand the Jesus child, and thus for a particular kind of Christianity. Ve brought fresh energy, a new attention to sights and sounds (which contributed to the later 'observer consciousness' of English empiricism) and a language which dispensed with complexities like gender and declension to become modern English. From these seafarers derived the future mercantile element, English common law, and the qualities of the English gentleman.[68]

The Franks under the inspiration of Vili overlept the Celts of western Germany to reach Gaul in 470. Vili (will) bore the sun forces that work with form, understanding and movement, which brought about the new mobility of soul needed for the awakening there shortly of the intellectual soul. The Franks had a tendency to war and politics. They too settled in village communities and replaced blood bonds by bonds to the soil, forming a balance with the original European blood. They expanded rapidly after the accession of Clovis in 481, whose conversion to Rome in 496 marked a major turning point. But such incomprehensible dogmas as 'the identity of Father and Son, co-equal and co-eternal' could only be implanted superficially as articles of faith with Roman force—hardly true Christianity. It was however a necessity that the Arian union of the sense-perceptible with the cosmic-spiritual in each individual should everywhere be eliminated for a time, and this was overlaid by Roman language, customs and beliefs.[69]

In Scandinavia most people were still childlike, with a few God-intoxicated individuals wandering as teachers. But one tribe, probably from Bergund, swept south to occupy what became Burgundy. Their path was crossed by Vandals, untouched by Christianity, who passed right across Austria, Spain and North Africa to reach Carthage in 429, from where they attacked Rome by sea. Meanwhile the

Huns had pressed through Russia and reached Hungary in 425. Their compact unity and—in the eyes of European Christians—almost idolatrous submission to Attila made them an irresistible terror. By 451 their army was outside Paris, but they were turned by the Franks to Italy. Confronted by the Pope, Attila did not know the power of Christianity, now reinforced by Arianism, and buckled before it. By 468 they were back in Russia. In Poland the Slavs were at this time emerging as separate peoples from the common Slav-Germanic stock.[70]

The Roman Empire had already become too large, and now that it could conquer nothing more it went to pieces. The demand of the legions in the East for coin had undermined life in Rome, but the Goths were unused to money and hence unaffected. The Empire fell in 476, and Theodoric the Ostrogoth (473–526) ruled from Ravenna, where we owe to him the magnificent mosaics.[71]

Through all these vast movements and settlements, though small in numbers by today's standards, the Germanic soul element was sacrificed on the altar of mankind, and a common physical blood-stock disseminated by intermarriage across the whole of central and western Europe. Those, however, who remained behind in Germany retained a certain inner malleability (evidenced in the consonantal sound-shifts of their language) which was to be fertile ground for future developments.[72]

During the central third of the intellectual or mind soul period, the Church established dogmas that pushed spiritual reality into a beyond, and engendered the belief that one should not and cannot reflect on the supersensible, the sphere to which the Mystery of Golgotha belongs. It thus became an institution for *not* understanding the Mystery of Golgotha. But in the Germanic peoples this Mystery was absorbed through a living element that was, however, devoid of wisdom.[73]

4
THE JUPITER REGENCY OF ZACHARIEL— THE DAWN OF PERSONAL INTELLIGENCE
Sixth to mid-ninth century

The Quality of Jupiter

The name Zachariel ('God remembers') is not used in other contexts by Steiner.

Jupiter is the guardian of the cosmic thoughts ordering the solar system, which resound as cosmic choral music and give meaning and content to the Harmony of the Spheres. It is the realm of the Spirits of Wisdom, and hence the radiant origin of wisdom.[74] In revealing the cosmic thoughts of the universe, Jupiter is the source on the one hand of the laws of nature and on the other hand of the inner will impulse active when we think them.[75]

Jupiter spirits seethe in the human nervous system, either through the twelve sensory nerves into the brain or through the breathing and solar plexus into the spinal cord. These spirits stand behind the capacity to distinguish truth from semblance, the essential from the inessential, based on the two-petal lotus flower in the forehead. Jupiter thus brings about the soul mood of logicism, which enables thoughts, ideas and concepts to be connected into a thought-organism. At the same time it protects us from dissolving into the light-ether.[76]

The sphere delimited by Jupiter is known as the oceanic region of Spirit-land, where after death the flowing thoughts are recognized to be the earthly experience of universal life. This evokes both reverence for the unity and harmony of the universe that lies at the basis of religion, and awareness that individual destiny is inseparable from that of the community. This all-encompassing quality is characterized by the vowel 'O'.[77]

In the lower organism Jupiter works into the liver as the centre of life. It also reveals our inclinations of temperament and sympathies. The Jupiter Mysteries are perceived through looking back onto the period of maturity between 49 and 56. The peoples of Europe are specially subject to the forces of Jupiter (Zeus), and are distinguished from one another by the preponderant activity of one or other of the senses.[78]

Celtic Christianity

The Hibernian Mysteries, which were specially connected with the balance between scientific truth and artistic phantasy in relation to the origin and future of the earth, here enter recorded history. The Irish monasteries developed a community life which combined prayer, intellectual effort and manual work. They inherited a wisdom concerning the etheric cosmos, now permeated by the resurrected Christ as the redeemer of elemental nature, and laid special emphasis on the Trinity and the Angelic host. But they also studied both Plato and Aristotle in the original Greek (which had been known there since pre-Christian times). In the first centuries Irish monks had carried impulses similar to those of Pelagius as far as Alsace. Then in the second half of the sixth century men like Columba (563–97) and Columbanus (590–615)—and 278 are known by name—carried learning and Celtic Christianity to Scotland and as far as northern Italy. Gregorian chant was introduced in 577. The monastic Rule of Columba, based on penances and fasting, was much more severe than the later Benedictine Rule still in use.[79]

In Wales the Celtic Church was similarly created out of the Arthurian Mysteries, mainly by Dyfrig (Dubricius, 500–37), and then disseminated by David (*c.* 550). The Celtic Church did not, however, work in Anglo-Saxon England, still at the tribal stage, where rare traces of Christianity survived from the Roman occupation. It was proseletized from Rome by Augustine in 597 and submitted in 664.

Odile, a blind girl from Alsace, was five times threatened with death for her faith. In 666 her inner eye was opened to life beyond birth and death, and she founded a convent from which trouvères are said to have carried to Troyes the legend of Perceval later used by Chrestien, in which the Grail is a source of spiritual nourishment and the object of a quest. The 'Great Book of the Grail' was written in 'bright Britain'—probably Brittany—in 750, and describes the Grail as a little book of supreme wisdom in Christ's own hand that outlined a path of initiation, offered by Him to a lone hermit between Easter and Whitsun. The Grail Mystery was at this time the Christianized form of esoteric wisdom from the age of the sentient soul. The main Irish legends were recorded in the sixth century, and the epic of Beowulf from the Northern Mysteries in England followed in 715.[80]

Eastern Christianity

Meanwhile the Orthodox Church flourished alongside the Byzantine Empire, culminating in the Santa Sophia (532), Church of the Divine Wisdom and reputed home of Our Lady. A sublime esotericism still lived in its cult, and up to the tenth century the priest still met in the Mass spiritual beings as real as human beings, the Intelligences of the Cosmos. Incomprehensible to the intellect, but penetrated with ardent devotion, this worked with power. It was not, however, destined to enter the West. After Justinian had in the service of opposing powers closed the Greek schools of philosophy in 529, Orthodoxy saw itself not only as the defender of the true faith that had originated in the East but also as bearer of the heritage of Greek culture. The cross with Christ upon it appeared first in this sixth century. And now that memory was less trustworthy, the transmitted teachings of Dionysius the Areopagite (successor to St Paul in his esoteric school), which concerned especially the Divine Hierarchies, were recorded in debased form as the work of the Pseudo-Dionysius.[81]

In Bulgaria the Bogomils ('beloved of God') had since the fifth century been spreading the teaching of Manes, despite persecution and destruction of all their documents by the Byzantine Church. Then Christian Bulgars were driven from Ukraine into Bulgaria in 675, forcing the Bogomils in turn to Bosnia, and permanently severing the South Slavs from the East Slavs in Russia. The Bulgars still experienced nature with its aura as the realm of the Father, but they were also specially aware of the spirits of good and evil in the soul and were regarded as heretics by the Orthodox.[82]

The Arabic Impulse

The last representatives of Aristotelian and Platonic wisdom in Athens exiled by Justinian made their way via Antioch and Syria to Jundi Sabur in Persia, where the teachers were inspired by luciferic-ahrimanic powers (known in the Apocalypse by the symbol 666). The aim of the latter was to make the human being entirely dependent on his personality. They sought to bestow in 666 as a kind of revelation all the knowledge which is to be mastered gradually up to the middle of the spiritual soul age (AD 2500) through scientific experiment. This would have cut off all subsequent evolution and bound people to the earth. It was a phenomenon of great power, highly dangerous for mankind, and preparations were made to deluge the whole of the then 'civilized' world with this learning.

But through the forces brought by Christ 333 years before the midpoint of the whole post-Atlantean age the evil 333 years after it was averted. A fantastic intellectual culture did arise there, where the descent of the Cosmic Intelligence was first completed, and the intellectual soul fully awoke. All the wisdom brought from Greece was studied with great diligence, and mathematics and science were developed. But retarded spiritual forces, though forming an opposition to the Christ-impulse, deadened the effect. For Mohammed and his visionary religious teachings stole the ground from under its feet, so that it could achieve nothing.[83]

Mohammed founded Islam in 612 as a synthesis of the wisdom-teachings of Egypt, Chaldea and especially the Jehovah moon-religion. But everything connected with clairvoyant perception was discarded in favour of dependence entirely on reason and intellectual thinking. Old concepts were thus recast into the abstract forms of Arabic science and the service of Allah. Moslem thought gave the final impulse to logical thinking, which is incapable of rising to what is spiritual. We see this in the Arabesque, which cannot rise to what is living but remains formal—the spirit is sucked out.[84]

Now the Arabic host, inspired by a Spirit of Personality, spread westwards, took Jerusalem in 636, surged across North Africa, and carried Islam into Spain in 711. There they defeated the Visigoths and drove north until thrown back by the Franks under Martel in 732. Thereafter they controlled Spain (except Galicia) to a decreasing extent for 250 years. Moorish cities became centres of scientific work, incorporating works of Aristotle hitherto unknown in the West. The experience of these people was: 'I feel, I will, but thoughts are breathed into us all from the sub-lunary sphere at birth and return there at death, continuing to work in the cosmic ether.' This highly stimulating intellectual thinking spread through the monasteries of Europe, especially in Ireland, from the seventh century onwards, enriching through the interchange of thought the Christian culture that had spread north of the Mediterranean—although a weakening of conscience was associated with it. Acquisition by the Arabs of the technique of paper-making from China in 751 further enhanced their influence.[85]

Chalibert, grandfather of Charlemagne, is said to have gone east in 765 to rescue before the reign of Harun-al-Rashid (803–13) certain ideas of Aristotle concerning substance and form which would provide the basis to understand the transubstantiation of bread and wine in the eucharist, which is at the basis of Christianity. The creative forces of the bread represented the interplay between the star forces concentrated in the sun and the earth forces; and the wine represented the healing forces working in the blood. Both were experienced as expressions of the Father, but the experience had become decadent and was in future only to be grasped through the 'I'.[86]

Charlemagne

The Frankish kingdom was expanding into Germany and Italy, the latter a gift to the Pope as temporal ruler. The Germanic mystery centre at the Externsteine, a sun-temple on rocky pinnacles with a rune of the sun in the cave below, had been closed by Boniface of Exeter, and the 'pillar of Irmin' reputed to reach to Asgard, the home of the gods, was cast down in 750. The aim of Charlemagne (771–814) was to reimpose the Roman Empire and its Church, and he thought of Christianity as the means to political power. His dynasty was said to derive from the Niebelungen on Atlantis, who held both priestly and worldly power.

Through his campaigns most of the Arian peoples perished, and Arianism died out. But he did secure northern Spain against the Moors, thus protecting the Sierra de la

Demanda with the Grail castle and the route of spiritual pilgrimage to Compostella. Frankish priests of the time were relatively uneducated, so Charlemagne called scholars from all directions as teachers and leaders. Fiery monks from Ireland and Scotland brought holy inspiration and religious zeal, and encouraged spiritual striving in the service of mankind; and Alcuin from England became a close adviser.[87]

In 800 Charlemagne was crowned by the Pope—but to his wrath as Emperor, for he did not accept the Pope's authority to do this, and it provoked opposition from the existing Emperor in Constantinople. He was called at this time 'Father of Europe', which did not include Britain, Islamic Spain or the Slavic east. In 813 he established a Michael festival to be celebrated throughout his realm. In him exoteric and esoteric Christianity were united.

With the increasing individuality of the time, Spirits of Language, Archai working as Archangels, were separating out the vernacular languages of Italian, Spanish and French, with their pronouns and auxiliary verbs, from the ubiquitous Latin, and also Welsh from the British language and the Slav tongues from Slavonic. At Charlemagne's death in 814 his empire was divided on a hereditary basis into France, Germany and Italy by the first trilingual document known. By 843 it had collapsed.

In 846 Arabs from Sicily sacked Rome, and Latin political power vanished. About this time Moravians, Czechs, Slovaks and Southern Slavs were Christianized—the Slovenes with the help of an Irish bishop. In the Germanic poem 'Heliand' (830) Jesus is portrayed as a German duke, his disciples as a tribal assembly, and the saints as heroes.[88]

Yet another impulse was afoot. In 793 marauding Vikings from Norway reached the east coast of England, and by 835 had brought most of the monastic culture of Ireland to an end. With the courageous will developed in the Northern Mysteries, they also swarmed and settled around the coasts of France. They were organized round the closer family and the grouping of families, with a 'prince' who dominated the group. About the same time their neighbours the Varengians of Sweden went south-east into Russia. The principal god of both was Thor/Donar/Perun, lord of thunder and lightning, who was felt as bestowing the individual ego out of the tribal ego. More thoughtful and contemplative than the Vikings, the Varengians were everywhere absorbed by Slavs, Tartars and Mongolians; nothing but the name given them by the Finns—Ruotsi, Ros, Russians—remained. In due course they were to meet the Vikings in Constantinople, thus encircling Europe. They also completed another circle of a spiritual nature, formed by the impulse of Christ that flowed from Jerusalem to the monasteries of Ireland—the impulse of the Hibernian and Arthurian Mysteries, which reached from Ireland and Cornwall to northern Russia, and the subsequent flow of pilgrims from northern Russia to the grave of the Redeemer.[89]

5
THE MERCURY REGENCY OF RAPHAEL—CHRISTENDOM (PERSONAL FEELING)
Mid-ninth to twelfth century

Raphael and the Quality of Mercury

As patron of Eastertide, Raphael ('God heals') stands as the great cosmic physician, with deep and thoughtful gaze, leaning on the staff of Mercury, supported by forces within the earth. In spring he works in nature, making possible a knowledge of the forces of healing, of resurrection, that stand between Lucifer and Ahriman. In autumn he regulates our breathing system, where the cosmic healing forces lie.[90]

Mercury is the master of combining thinking, which enables us to reflect on sense impressions and to form thoughts, while feeling echoes on. It works in the intellectual soul, leading human beings out of the sense world to the spiritual beings revealed in the stars. Mercury shines in the spiritual heaven with a wonderful glowing light, and we can be led by this messenger of the gods along true paths into the spiritual world, into understanding for the spiritual. This is the region of Soul Light, where after death a sensuous love of nature gives place to a search for the spirit in nature, where sociability depends on moral ideals, and longing for an earthly or heavenly paradise is overcome.[91]

Mercury nevertheless has an element of egoism, a luciferic tendency to be intellectual, to cleverness. For Lucifer actually has his home on Mercury (exoteric Venus, see p. 11). The soul mood of Mercury is transcendentalism, the feeling that the essence of things lies hidden in a sphere outside the soul's possibility of real experience. Earthly battles and conflicts are a copy of the continuing opposition between Michael and the luciferic aspect of Mercury. For the Mercury-sphere is the realm of the Archangels, the Folk Spirits; and Mercury builds through different nourishment the virtues and vices of the different national characters.[92]

The forces of Mercury affect the head and its thinking when it is in the new phase; the rhythmic system and especially the lungs as it waxes; the swinging limb movements when it is full; and the rhythmic system again as it wanes. The inner organ for the perception of the Mercury forces is our childhood between 7 and 14, when the breathing system must be brought into balance, and illness is at a minimum. It enables us to take hold of the solid constituents of the body. We have to approach individualities of this period like a child willing to learn from its teachers.[93]

Esoteric and Exoteric Christianity

We have seen how Christ lived especially in the hearts of the Arian Christians moving from east to west, and the zeal of the Celtic saints fired by cosmic wisdom coming from the west. The higher reality behind these facts is that the Spirit Self of Christ, the fully spiritualized soul forces, was spreading westwards from Palestine; and His Life Spirit, the fully spiritualized life forces in the realm of nature, was spreading eastwards from Ireland. And in the year 869 they met.

This momentous event was also expressed in the confluence of two mystery streams. The Arthurian stream, the last to be inspired by Michael, which carried star-wisdom from the megalithic age in humanized form, and had perceived how the elements were transformed by the event on

Golgotha, was completing its task. Its basic extant text, the tale of the Culhwch and Olwen, was probably first composed orally about 850. In contrast, the Grail stream had originated from the cup of the Last Supper, was developed in the light of Aristotle's work, and had been carried by Angels to 'Mont Salvat' in Spain. From the confluence of these two arose the new Christian initiation for the coming spiritual-soul age. This was expressed in the legend of the wounded Amfortas and the healing question of Parzival, who had to ask inwardly about the significance of the bread (star-wisdom) and wine (healing), the lily and the rose. Thereby the Spirit of Esoteric Christianity took up his task.[94]

Pope Nicholas I (858–67) held that Europeans, despite strong and healthy feelings, could not yet link concepts adequately to reach the spirit, and regarded both eastern and western esoteric streams as harmful to them. He accordingly denounced these streams, and turned instead to faith in a divinity transcending experience. Eastern ritual, hitherto an experience of the etheric body, he made into a mere symbol for eyes to see. And whereas the transubstantiation was previously accessible only to those specially prepared, now the whole Mass was made exoteric. The differences between Rome and Byzantium therefore became a permanent separation. Western esoteric wisdom related to the etheric cosmos he replaced by dogma and tales of the earthly deeds of Jesus.[95] The masses were thereby prevented from receiving the real substance of religious culture, which was kept far more secret than it ever was in ancient occult schools. And all knowledge of the nature of Christ's divinity had been lost. Thus the Church was no longer founded on the Mystery of Golgotha—the supersensible was driven out, and the most active element left was the forms and ceremonies that came from the age of the sentient soul. From this evolved 'The People of the Church' for whom Christ is an invisible king.[96]

The descent of the Cosmic Intelligence was now established in the West, and the intellectual soul was fully aware of the subjective aspect of thinking. But because the fact that thought at the same time manifests a spiritual reality was not understood, the eighth Ecumenical Council, also in 869, denied the reality of spirit, formulating as dogma that the soul merely has spiritual qualities. This was a direct result of the impulse of Jundi Sabur, and in turn determined the whole character of modern thinking, especially that of science.[97]

At the same time the Planetary Archangels other than Michael—led by Oriphiel, inspirer of the impulse of Rome—observed the fall of the Intelligence and the increasing sunspots. They resolved no longer to be ruled by the sun, but to make the earth directly dependent on the entire cosmos. Michael, however, was determined to lead humanity back to the guidance of the sun. Thus they came into opposition, and many Angels left the sun-sphere to live on earth in communion with the planetary Spirits, while others remained with Michael on the sun. This of necessity brought the karma of the human beings connected with the two groups into social disorder.

With the founding of Cluny in 910—eventually mother of 1400 abbeys—began the great explosion of monastic life, which started as a protest at the politicizing of Christianity. But withdrawal from the world harks back to the ancient East and Lucifer, and is foreign to true Christianity. Everywhere the clergy worked with suggestion rather than explanation, which crept into human souls. Many pilgrimages were made to the Holy Land, Compostella or closer shrines, bringing people together from many lands, often with Latin as a common language. After celibacy was imposed in 965, the cult of the Virgin spread widely.

In England, Alfred (871–99) and his daughter Ethelfled (883–918) freed the south and west from Viking incursions by founding many urban centres, combining administration, trade, defence and a Christianizing influence of justice and humanity—but their civilizing impulse did not survive them.

In 906 the Magyars had moved into Hungary, causing widespread terror until again stopped by the Franks, whose cavalry became the origin of knighthood. The Holy Roman Empire of the German Nation was re-established in 962, but Henry II (865) sought both spiritual deepening and his freedom from Rome—an early hint towards the Reformation—because the Pope felt himself not only as representative of Christ but as a temporal lord. Meanwhile, along the trade routes from the Orient came such impulses as alchemy, astrology and divination. The growing towns were being transformed from fortresses to trading centres, where personality could unfold. A Masonic assembly in York is recorded in 926.[98]

Russians and Normans

The Varengians from Sweden passed through the Finns (who expressed the threefold nature of the soul in the *Kalevala* and in their Primary Chronicle) and in 862 reached Novgorod, already a democratic state with economic links to the Baltic and an emphasis on thinking. They then passed through a group of small aristocratic princedoms dominated by feelings ranging from sanctity to wild passions. In Kiev they found a theocratic state with special reverence for Father Sun and Mother Earth, forming the centre of twelve tribes of East Slavs. They continued to Georgia, where Byzantine monks steered them to Mount Athos. After immersion in Orthodoxy they reached Constantinople, and carried Byzantine Christianity back to Kiev, where it was chosen over other religions for the spiritual reality of its ritual. But Kiev developed its own Slavonic liturgy and kept Byzantium at arm's length. Russians experienced Christ with particular intensity, receiving the revelation of the

Christ-impulse directly as an ever-present inner aura which impregnated their thinking and feeling. Receptive to His continuous 'breath', they became what may be called the 'People of Christ'.[99]

Poland was converted in 966, Denmark in the eleventh and Finland in the twelfth century. In the Balkans, Cyril developed in the ninth century a Slav alphabet (Cyrillic), and Methodius founded a Slav Church which defended the Spirit as third Person of the Trinity, despite opposition from Rome.

Meanwhile the Danes harried England, and established the Kingdom of Canute and his son (1016–42). The Norsemen who had settled in France were rapidly transformed by the thinking element of the intellectual soul in the Roman Church to become known as Normans, and in exchange actively strengthened the will of the Franks. In 1066 they conquered England and South Wales, deeply despising the Anglo-Saxons who still lived in the sentient soul. While accepting the Pope spiritually, William denied that England was a papal fief.

Norsemen had also reached Greenland in 896 and North America in 1100. As Normans they conquered central Italy in 1017, and pressed on to Greece (1147) and thence to Constantinople. In Central Europe, still largely of Celtic and Gothic blood, the feeling of being encircled is important even in the twentieth century as an essential ingredient in Germanic ego-development.

The New Millennium

Every thousand years, when the millennium approaches, Lucifer and Ahriman are able in conjunction to make a particularly strong attack on human progress, because things are pictured too emphatically in terms of space and time. At the end of the first millennium an alliance between

Klingsor (Ahriman) in the toe of Italy and Iblis (Lucifer) in Sicily created a centre of the most extreme forces of occult evil. This area today is the centre of the Mafia.[100]

After the millennium arrived without the end of the world, as widely feared, it was seen as a turning-point for Europe. Vikings, Magyars, Russians were Christianized and brought within western culture. Compostella was freed from the Moors in 1018 and the rest of Spain by 1097. The great school of Chartres was founded in 1028, where the Seven Liberal Arts were taught as a path of initiation through the planetary spheres; and it was possible to speak of the elementary world, the relation of the planets to the soul, and that of the zodiac to the ego. But increasingly the goddess Natura, the embodiment of such wisdom, eluded them, to their great sadness. In Ireland and Spain too a few schools had survived where Christ could still be understood through spiritual vision. But by 1050 energy turned to the great period of cathedral building and Romanesque art, and in the twelfth century nearly every major church was rebuilt.[101]

Pope Gregory (1073–85) thought the Church could not err, and that he had authority from Christ to depose emperors; his reforms met strong opposition. As Cluny became rich its emphasis on manual labour lapsed, and it lost lustre. The Carthusians (1098) and Cistercians (1099) kept a more severe regime, including silence. Bernard of Citeaux (1113–53) was a tireless traveller, pious and ascetic, a diplomat and a real European; through him innumerable feelings were turned towards the humanity of Jesus.

The old world had in one sense come to an end, for Anselm's proof of God's existence (1109) shows that people no longer experienced God. It was an age of doubt, in which the intellectual soul sought understanding through cleverness. Scholasticism began to impose a severe thought-discipline on both men and women. It relied on razor-sharp intelligence of astonishing acumen, but was still a manifestation of the Angel or group soul 'on high', not yet under full human control. The technique of Abelard (1115–42) of disputation 'for and against' reached verbal consistency, but never a knowledge of reality. What worked here was only the garment of a thought element from Roman times.[102]

The Roman concept of hierarchy had grown into the Norman concept of hereditary feudalism, service in exchange for protection—but the protection was often not given. Most communities were still small, landowners oppressive, clergy illiterate. Bishops dominated civil government through Roman law, and the Church laid claim to all knowledge, but it was an abstraction clothed in Latin which hovered above people's heads. The first universities were founded in Bologna in 1158, Oxford in 1167 and Paris in 1179.

Nevertheless a very rich spiritual life developed throughout Europe among the peasantry, permeated by the gods of locality and an element of magic. Reverence for nature was virtually unchanged, elemental beings of flower and forest were a reality, and thoughts about nature were felt as if something real took possession of the intellect. Moreover people had constant inklings and premonitions arising from the rhythmic system, and spoke of them. These were always connected with riddles put by the spiritual world, or tasks which required cleverness or skill to achieve. This lived alongside the economic and social life of the village and Gospel teaching. All over western Europe towns were however developing, to which people from the villages brought this lively inner life—but then their thinking tended to become intellectual. A new class of tradesmen and artisans arose, and in the guilds there was a strong sense of freedom and personal value. It was just 2160 years after the first urban culture of Greece. History was moving fast, with new forms of society, new organizations, laws and conditions of life. Arabic, Irish, Arthurian and

Grail legends and stories helped keep souls alive. And there were still theologians, alchemists and others who knew for certain of body, soul and spirit.[103]

The Crusades

In 1090 Turks appeared between the Danube and the Balkans. They were among those descended from the Turanians, who in the central period of Atlantis had betrayed the Mysteries, causing the eventual submergence. They had migrated to central Asia, with a degenerate clairvoyance, their shamans practising lower magic—even black magic. In the fourth and fifth millennia BC the Iranians, servants of Ahura Mazdao, had fought against them one of the greatest wars ever known. Mellowed now by Islam, but influenced by a backward Spirit of Form, they took Jerusalem in 1076 and maltreated pilgrims. The response of Europe was the Crusades (1095–1272). These were actually started to found a Christianity based on Jerusalem instead of Rome, whereas the Church used them to renew its own strength. Many freemen, even nobility, were already vagrant and keen to serve; others went in search of salvation or forgiveness. Though taken up with religious emotionalism, the physical goal of the empty grave replaced the spiritual goal of inner experience. Jerusalem was freed, but not for long (1099–1187). Germanic and Romance peoples however met, Moorish science was disseminated, and many secrets of oriental medicine were brought back. But the impulse was fundamentally a turning back to the past.[104]

A select band of knights under Godfrey of Bouillon had resided in Solomon's temple, and in 1118 the Order of the Knights Templar was founded. They brought home the use of loan money, an anathema to the Church. But they had such an absolute devotion to Christ and to the Mystery of Golgotha, to their Order and to its task, that many experienced a real Christian initiation—including visions of Lucifer, Ahriman and other spiritual beings—which was before its due time. The Knights of St John were concerned mainly with hospital and medical care. The Teutonic Knights, despite massacring the heathen Balts, developed there a constitution with an elected ruler. Most other knights lapsed into an empty court life, enlivened by the vernacular love lyrics of the troubadours; and the pursuit of love took not only idealistic but extravagant forms. The powerful citizen class continued to emerge, and manufactures flourished. Even Dante (1292–1321) and Giotto (1297–1330) were still under the influence of Raphael.[105]

6
THE MARS REGENCY OF SAMAEL—CORPORATE AND PERSONAL WILLING
Thirteenth to fifteenth century

Samael and the Mars Quality

The Archangel Samael ('God hears') is otherwise named by Steiner only in esoteric studies, as a luciferic being who draws forth from us the destructive, pernicious forces of the Double—but this enables us to see and overcome them. Mars liberates us from personality and blood ties.[106]

Mars is traditionally the god of war, who brings us strength, but is aggressive, a cosmic agitator. In this aspect it works in the gall, which prepares the bile to transform the substances we eat. The corresponding soul mood is voluntarism, which regards the whole of reality as a manifestation of will, whether as a unit or a host of separate entities. It works further through the iron in the blood, which holds together our warmth organism as foundation for the ego.[107]

In the upper organism the Mars forces work into the larynx, giving us the freedom to speak of what is good or less good. The Dynamis or Spirits of Motion are active here from the realm of creative ringing, the sphere of Cosmic Speech. Mars is thus involved in our everyday relations with other people.[108]

The Mars-sphere is the 'continental' region of Spirit-land, which contains the archetypes of everything physical, including the inorganic in plant, animal and man, which appears spiritually as voids shaped from without. It is the life-filled thought workshop where lifeless things are formed. Through the 16-petal lotus flower in the larynx it enables us to gain deeper insight into the laws of natural phenomena. Experience between death and rebirth of the Mars forces of materialism, which reached a climax in the sixteenth century, gave rise to natural-scientific thinking.[109]

Before 1250

At the beginning of the thirteenth century an important exchange of ideas took place in the supersensible world between the teachers of Chartres who had just died and those about to incarnate in the Dominican Order, concerning the future development of the Michael-impulse both on earth and in the spiritual world up to the nineteenth century. Then in 1217 the Dominicans were founded, on the basis of outstanding intellectual education. The Franciscans too were founded in 1220 as itinerant preachers by the loving Francis of Assisi (previously a pupil of the Buddha), and the Carmelites (1224) who were also medicants. The Church thus strengthened its grip as a powerful universalist impulse, using the susceptibility of people to suggestions that are not fully understood. Cathedrals and churches were still being built, now lyrical rather than classical in style.[110]

Views contrary to dogma were now intolerantly and forcibly suppressed. In Italy and southern France the Albigenses, followers of Manes, claimed the right to teach from the Gospels (1167), but the Church, wanting to keep these as a secret source of authority, and fearing contradictions with dogma, forbade this and launched a crusade to stop it (1181–1218). The Cathars, more extreme, were repeatedly attacked from 1209 to the slaughter of Montsegur in 1244. The Inquisition, the great torturer and burner of books, was directed against them, and the persecution of witches began. New texts of Aristotle from Islam were banned in 1215, but they could not be suppressed. The same year was promulgated the dogma of transubstantiation, that bread and wine are physically changed in the eucharist into the actual body and blood of Christ. The inner experience described on page 47 had been lost. In 1225 the works of Scotus Erigena were condemned to be burned—he had himself been burned in 896 because, still using the etheric brain, he thought differently on this subject, and on freedom of the will.[111]

Nevertheless it was still possible to undergo initiation: to experience on a mountain-top the youthful forces of the etheric body flowing from the cosmos; to experience down a mine the ageing forces of the astral body from the earth's depths; and to experience the stages of the evolution of the earth in terms of the three Hierarchies, with Man as the fourth. Moreover, important remnants of esotericism were being recorded physically for the future in such works as the *Elder Edda* (1194), the *Niebelungenlied* (1200), Eschenbach's *Parzival* (1210) and others.[112]

Suddenly in 1222, surging across Europe like an elemental phenomenon of nature, the Mongol hordes appeared. In the Mongoloid race, descended from the decadent seventh culture of Atlantis, Mars spirits worked in the blood against the progressive Elohim. For Lucifer, having failed on Atlantis and in Greece to lead souls away to his own kingdom, charged Genghis Khan (1210–27) to change the imaginations of Europe back into old visionary forms—but this too failed. They were perceived as the judgment of God, and had they triumphed the fright of European souls would have disinclined them to reincarnate, wiping out western culture. But there was a counterpart quite evidently spiritual: after they had occupied Hungary and Bohemia a spiritual wall was erected by the Spirit of Esoteric Christianity (previously the Celtic Archangel) together with the Spirits of Form (who had inspired human imaginations); and in 1242 the Mongols withdrew to Russia.[113] However Russia (except Novgorod) had until 1480 to take this karma upon itself, with all its consequences—otherwise it would have developed much faster. Overland trade, and the spiritual concepts that travelled with it, were at first interrupted. The Mongols, however, restored the trade using silver coin. And the Hanseatic League (1230), formed by merchants on the Baltic coast, was defended by the Teutonic Knights, who again sought to impose Christianity by the sword. Central European peasants meanwhile infiltrated and colonized the Slav territory of eastern Europe. The southern road to China was opened by Marco Polo's great journey of 1271–95.[113b]

Up to the thirteenth century there had been a lively traffic with northern America via Ireland and Iceland, and medical and other herbs were imported. But to protect Europe from subterranean forces of evil affecting the subconscious especially strongly there—seen later in the enhanced greed for gold—until the consciousness soul was ready to withstand them, Rome made every effort to stop this, so that America was for a while forgotten.[114]

Then in the 1240s a group was formed around Christian Rosencreutz, whose members bore in their persons all the wisdom of the seven ages of Atlantis and that of the post-Atlantean times; the totality of ancient wisdom was thus brought into a single focus. Thereafter around 1250 there was for a while no clairvoyance at all on the earth. During a period of twilight consciousness, physical facts were seen as spiritual Imaginations, while the spiritual world was depicted as physical fact.[115]

End of the Intellectual or Mind Soul Age

The second half of the thirteenth century brought the great battle between Realism and Nominalism to a climax.

Realists still experienced the cosmic creative forces (*universalia ante rem*) which create the forms of nature (*universalia in re*) as also shaping their thoughts (*universalia post rem*). But the Nominalists had no such experience; for the abstract thinking of Neoplatonism and an education based only on grammar and rhetoric could only see thoughts as names made up in human heads; and because the Cosmic Intelligence had descended to humanity, the Arab idea of thoughts as part of the world ether was no longer true to experience. The Dominicans especially attacked the Arabic view with inner fire as heresy, and defended with sharp incisive thought the individuality who made the effort to think. The main defenders of Realism were Albertus Magnus (1265–80) and Thomas Aquinas (1259–74). Thomas quoted in his works from 27 Councils of the Church, but never from that of 869 which had denied the spirit. He recognized himself as existing within his soul life and therefore able to explore it. He concluded that there are some divine truths which can only be received by inner revelation.

Since the ninth century the spirit had flashed forth in Germanic souls, and it was the quest for such revelations, which united the soul with the divine, that was undertaken by the German mystics Eckhardt (d. 1329), Tauler (d. 1361) and Suso (d. 1365). But they spoke so deeply from the heart that the Church branded them as heretics. Raymond Lull (1260–1315) still spoke of the Mysteries of the Word. The mind soul was at this time still permeated by heartfelt reverence and piety.[116]

In sharp contrast, Roger Bacon (1249–77) demanded that science be based only on sense-observation and experiment, thus excluding the spirit and establishing the materialistic thinking in science that flowed on until today, supported by the universities. This 'impartial' scientific thinking derives in fact from Jundi Sabur, via Avicenna (d. 1037) and Averroes (1145–98). It has nothing to do with Christianity.[117]

In 1309 occurred something which would have been inconceivable a century earlier—Philip IV of France 'kidnapped' the Pope from Rome to Avignon. Catholic power was waning. At Philip's behest the Pope dissolved the Templars in 1312, and their leader was burned at the stake in 1314. Philip was filled with envy for their gold, but because they worked with loans it did not exist as he expected. In eradicating them under torture, which distorted their clairvoyance and evoked false confessions, he was a tool of opposing powers. This was completed in 1332 (2 × 666). Elsewhere the Templars continued in other forms. And after death their impulse worked down for 500 years through various occult lodges in opposition to Rome; but the dead hand of traditions from the third post-Atlantean epoch such as Masonic ritual emasculated progress there.[118]

In 1306 a league of European states was proposed by Dubois, with a permanent court of justice to impose trade sanctions or deportation on any disturber of the peace, but the age was not ready for this. There were hidden intentions to spread a generalized concept of what a state should be, but this would have annihilated the individuality of the different peoples too soon.

In England severe famine during 1315–17 followed by the Black Death during 1347–50 nearly halved the population. Feudalism loosened, Parliament rejected papal interference (1301–53), and with the division into two houses in 1341 democracy was beginning. The intermittent Hundred Years War between France and England began in 1336, in which artillery was used. In Scotland, still at the primitive stage of tribal (clan) warfare, Robert Bruce was fighting 'for freedom, for that alone which no honest man gives up but with life itself' (1320)—finally with success, but shortlived. In 1372 government there devolved on the 'Three Estates'—prelates, barons (administration and justice) and burgesses (providing finance).

An alternative Pope was eventually elected in Rome (the Great Schism, 1378), and a third in Pisa (1409–15). The mystical body of the Church was clearly corrupted, which the ending of scholasticism and the failure to complete cathedrals confirmed.

The Consciousness or Spiritual Soul Age Begins

At this time the First Hierarchy—Seraphim, Cherubim and Thrones—carried the Cosmic Intelligence from human hearts, into which it had descended, to the nerve-sense system, the head organization. By such a deed, the like of which had not occurred since Atlantean times, mankind was utterly transformed, though this only gradually became apparent. At the same time the Archangels who had guided human groups through blood-relationships withdrew to the nervous system, leaving the Angels to work more independently in the blood.[119]

In 1413 the new age of the consciousness soul or spiritual soul also began—the first such change for 2160 years. This is the soul which, freed from likes and dislikes, is to become conscious through its own effort of its true spiritual-cosmic nature. The being who is to be the new Spirit of the Age had since the twelfth century been rising from among the Archangels guiding the Germanic peoples, but for a long time leadership was still chiefly in the hands of the Archangels, who in many cases became servants of the Christ Spirit of the Age. For Michael was then working in the Sun-sphere, gathering up all that had once lived in the ancient Sun Mysteries, and expressing it again with untold significance to all whom he gathered round him—Angels, human beings, elemental beings—in a Supersensible School that continued through the sixteenth and seventeenth centuries. On earth there was an ahrimanic counterpart, which was responsible in 1454 for perhaps the most significant of all inventions—that of printing. As people sought their culture in print, instead of in paintings and sculptures equally accessible in church to all, an educated class developed, creating the social chasm with all its consequences.[120]

Only now were there people who thought totally with the physical brain. Their thoughts were mere established beliefs and traditions void of spiritual reality. But these shadowy images were felt to be justified because their content came from without, and could master the laws of inorganic nature. But they have no influence on the will, which fell back on instincts, and here Ahriman takes hold. Materialism now began in earnest—natural science, social theory, industrial techniques and a finance economy (stimulated by borrowings from the curia) all start to establish roots. The age of intellectualism, as distinct from intellectuality, unfolds.[121]

But—very importantly—in the Folk stream, as a result of the riddle-solving in the dreamy inklings of previous centuries, there was born for the very first time a thinking fully achieved through subjective activity, manifest chiefly in interpreting the phenomena of nature. The villages, supported by their landowners, now stood in opposition to the towns, which were centres of Roman administration. This in due course led to the Reformation. The first smouldering is seen in Wyclif (1366–84), who had translated the Bible into English and had dared to denounce the dogma of physical transubstantiation as incomprehensible. His view was condemned by the Pope in 1413. There followed the *Imitatio Christi* of à Kempis (1414) and the burning at the stake of Huss in 1416. In Holland the nonconformist Brethren of the Common Life were founded in 1427, and in Germany the Primitive school of painters expressed similar ideals. In Poland, prospering from accepting Jewish refugees, a remarkable declaration was adopted concerning the 'mystery of love'. This was not yet a birth of new ideas, but the search for a new, autonomous relationship to the old ones. The Folk Spirits were demanding that human beings take the Bible into their own hands. But the Lollards, followers of Wyclif, were persecuted (1382–1413) and the folk spirituality (page 57) survived only as a faint glow under the surface.[122]

England and France, closely interwoven for 300 years, were now separated through Joan of Arc (1428–31) under the inspiration of Michael. The broad idea of nationhood first emerged here. France gained free rein on the Continent, where personal freedom developed in the intellectual soul. England, forced back to its island, prepared to receive the consciousness soul by developing political freedom—people there wanted to take things into their own hands and parliamentary government emerged (1452–80)—and opened outwards to the whole world.

The Welsh were on the brink of independence in 1404 under Owain Glyn Dŵr, but did not succeed. The Wars of the Roses (1448–85) between York and Lancaster, behind which were deep spiritual forces, were yet small in scale. Symptomatically, Edward IV of York at his coronation (1461) reinstated an ancient ritual of adoration.[123]

The wonderful flowering of the Italian Renaissance (1434–1527) emancipated Italian consciousness from the papacy, but again turned back towards classical Rome and then to Greece. This was a necessity for Europe, despite its luciferic aspect. From the time of Giotto (1297–1330), who brought human figures from the gold to the blue sky, the genius of Italian painters had been incomparable, if sometimes too beautiful. The rise of portraiture in the towns expressed the strengthening of individuality. An esoteric centre—human, free and profound—was provided by the Medici court, especially by Ficino's hermetic Academy of Florence (1462–1521). Men such as Pico de Mirandola (1486–94) and Savonarola (d. 1498) still had direct vision of the spirit. Then in Leonardo (1480–1519), Raphael (1504–20) and Michelangelo (1497–1564) the spirit of the new age became clearly visible.[124]

The Rosicrucian brotherhood was founded in 1459, when Christian Rosencreutz (d. 1484) was 80. To gain their wisdom one had first to recognize the gentle radiance in the eyes of a hermit. There was then widespread an intense fear of all spiritual knowledge, and in a simple gathering of Rosicrucians esoteric knowledge of the cosmos was solemnly offered up in sacrifice on behalf of mankind, so that individuals might later overcome the Fall and recover it out of themselves.[125]

Yet Agrippa of Nettesheim (1486–1535) was still able to describe mankind as the Intelligence of the Earth, whose true home, were it not for the Fall, would be on the sun. In the fifteenth and sixteenth centuries there were still initiates, who although not necessarily seers, presented to those in lower grades symbols which expressed deep truths if a little spiritual effort was expended on them.[126]

Political Developments

In 1422 the Turks, who took Serbia in 1389 and Bulgaria in 1396, surrounded Byzantium. The Byzantine Church temporarily submitted to Rome in 1439. But the revitalized Russian Church rejected this, and broke completely before Byzantium fell in 1453. The Russian soul, whether Nordic, Slav or Asian, had never really been at one with Byzantine Orthodoxy. Since 1389 Moscow had steadily extended its domain; it broke the social and economic independence of Novgorod by cunning, cruelty and excessive taxes from 1471 to 1495. By 1533 it dominated all Russia, and the Church hierarchy was forced to submit to the Tsar. The idea of a single centralized state was the spiritual heritage of the Mongol invasion.

Under Duke Dandolo (1433–1505), the incarnation of an

ahrimanic spirit, Venice accumulated enormous capital through trade with the East—including the exchange for metal coin of 1000 human beings, from whom descended the leaders of the later hordes entering Europe.[127]

National impulses became more active—national groups formed in the Vatican Council in 1413, and in the universities. Portugal separated in 1385, and the marriage of Ferdinand of Castile and Isabella of Aragon in 1469 and the final exclusion of the Moors in 1492 laid the foundations for a united Spain. France annexed Burgundy in 1477 and Provence in 1483. Switzerland, starting from three cantons in 1291 and five more in 1386, set in contrast an example to Europe when Nicholas von der Flüe accepted a multilingual basis in 1481.

As the Archangels worked into the nervous system, human beings began to make the whole earth their own. Henry the Navigator (1437–60) founded the Order of Christ with ex-Templar knights, and financed explorations with their money. In 1488 Diaz rounded the Cape to India. British fishermen, denied the right to fish cod off Iceland, turned secretly to Newfoundland waters and set up drying stations there about 1480. Columbus met Bristolians in Spain, and in 1492 made his much-publicized voyage, expecting to reach Xipangu (Japan) as described by Marco Polo. Within two years Spain and Portugal had agreed with the Pope how to share the New World, but failed to consult England. When the Europeans came under the influence of the strong American earth forces, the lure of gold began to provide a strong ahrimanic counterbalance to the earlier luciferic power of the Mongol impulse in the east.[128]

During the closing years of this period, monarchs all over Europe began to take absolute powers of direct rule, twist laws and customs to their own advantage for so-called 'reasons of state', by-pass parliaments (except to obtain money), break promises, and become heartless, hypocritical and cruel. War at enormous cost was eulogized as 'normal' and 'glorious'. Traditional Christianity had lost its hold on leading personalities. Yet all this served to liberate individual egos from the feudal structure.

Not until 1604 was a Mercury impulse of peace brought by the Buddha to the Mars-sphere, where he fulfilled a mission echoing that of Christ on earth, so that in future Mars forces should impel human beings before birth to work for spiritual aims.[129]

7
THE MOON REGENCY OF GABRIEL—PERSONAL EGOISM, NATIONAL EGOISM

Sixteenth century to 1879

Gabriel and the Moon Quality

Gabriel ('God has shown himself strong') is well known from the Annunciation. He is the Christmas Archangel, weaving with gesture of benediction in winter clouds and white robes of snow. In summer he is at man's side, bringing through the earth the shaping forces of nourishment. During these centuries he directed forces transforming the brain so that it could take up spiritual knowledge in the following period of Michael.[130]

The moon-sphere delimits the activity of Angels, who lead human beings to their new incarnation. Within the moon itself dwell those who were the primeval teachers of mankind, who radiate what comes from the universe beyond. Thus all divine beings have the moon as their eye for earthly events. But it is above all the dwelling of Jehovah, the Spirit of Form who brought wisdom to mankind. On its dark side dwell sacrificial Spirits of Wisdom who restrain the luciferic light reflected from the sun.[131]

The moon-sphere is the realm of kamaloca, with its four aspects of glowing desires, mobile sensitiveness, wishes, likes and dislikes; and much antipathy is present in the first of these. It gives rise to the forming of mental pictures, fantasy and imagination, and to the creative, productive capacity. In the consciousness soul it relates what has been worked over by the intellectual soul to deeds of waking life.

Where illusory ideas, mediums and somnambulists are active, astral moon-beings are present who incline people to wrong-doing, irritation and anger.[132]

The moon also contains hardening forces which would have brought the earth to dust had it remained here. It holds fast, retards, makes stiff, and creates forms. It thereby condenses dream-consciousness to growth forces, and regulates the movement of reproduction throughout the body and physical heredity. The inner organ for perceiving the moon-sphere is thus the period of infancy up to age 7, through the forces of which one moulds and directs one's life.[133]

The soul mood stirred by the moon is occultism, which envisages reality as imperceptible to the senses, whether consisting of spiritual entities or materialistic atoms.[134]

The Reformation

During the last two periods, thought still permitted religious revelation to exist alongside its own growing strength. This has begun to change. The impulse started north of the Alps by Wyclif and Huss grew into the Reformation, led by helping Archangels. Luther—still with experiences of the demonic which he couched in medieval terms, but presaging the future in the freedom of his individuality—was in 1517 incited by the debauchery of the papacy and the sale of indulgences (purporting to remit time in purgatory) to publish his theses. This was a first step to the self-realization of Central Europe. His Church, based on justification by faith alone, retained the Bible, the sacraments and the eucharist. (Unfortunately his translation of the Bible was in a pedantic, philistine idiom which interrupted the spiritual evolution of the German language.) There were parallel movements in Switzerland led by Zwingli (1525–31), who rejected all sacraments, and

Calvin (1532–49), who asserted predestination (from him derived Scottish Presbyterianism). What the reformers never understood was how the divinity of Christ was related to the humanity of Jesus. Their iconoclasm led to the destruction of thousands of ancient works of art. And much of the Reformation, significantly, depended on the use of printing.[135]

In England the Anglican Church resulted from a king's personal desires—the only Church ever founded on such a worldly basis. From this flowed the habit of later English thinkers of leaving religion aside, not dealing with it. Henry VIII was served by the luciferic Wolsey (1515), the truly Christian More (1529) and the ahrimanic Thomas Cromwell (1532). Thomas More firmly rejected the break with Rome, which gave the brotherhood of landowners whom he had pilloried in his *Utopia* (1516) the chance to bring about his death, including ritual dismemberment, but he long continued to work down from the spiritual world. The Bible was now to be in every church, in new versions (1525–39). The old pagan festivals of May Day, Harvest, All Souls and so on were incorporated.[136]

The Counter-Reformation

Charles I of Spain inherited Burgundy and the Netherlands in 1516 and through bribery became Emperor of the 'Holy Roman' (Austro-Hungarian) Empire in 1520, thus dominating the Continent; and the papacy depended heavily on him. Spain's dominion over central America was led by strong desires for gold, which was acquired through great cruelty to the natives, setting ever new ahrimanic temptations for its rulers; and the Counter-Reformation was financed by this gold.

The spiritual spearhead, however, was Jesuitism (founded in 1534). This was based on strict will exercises directed only to body and soul, which brought an ancient vitality back into thinking, onto which traditional revelations were superimposed. The rule of absolute submission to the Pope strengthened the will of the priests, so that it worked directly on the astral bodies of others, especially the primitive, as in the clerical state of Paraguay (1610). But this infringed freedom, and is morally inadmissible in the consciousness-soul age. Jesuits were in fact opposing the reality of Christ, and put forward Jesus as the tyrant of evolving humanity. The kingdom of God was dragged down as a spiritual militia in the temporal world, but Christ said 'My kingdom is not of this world'.[137]

Spanish catholicism did, however, give rise to the mysticism of Theresa (1555–75) and John of the Cross (1560–87). But in general, after the expulsion of the Moors and Jews in 1492, and with exceptions such as Cervantes (1585–1615) Spain remained at the level of the sentient soul.[138]

The Role of Nationhood

The peoples of Europe were always differentiated by dependence on the various physical senses; and since the consciousness soul develops through the transforming by the ego of the physical body, national divergencies now come to the fore. During the Gabriel period nationalism thus arose as a phenomenon of nature; it was essentially a form of egoism (hence luciferic) of the group based on heredity; but Ahriman, exerting all his power to gain mastery over the Cosmic Intelligence before the coming Michael age, took hold of it as one of his tools. The old Mars forces also continued to work strongly.[139]

Two nations which have different tasks may well have different judgements that are not merely conceptual differences but are for them iron necessities. Thus there can be conflicting interests, both of which must become manifest in order to complement one another. People within each Folk need to feel in every fibre that 'this must happen'; and others should not try to bring both within a common consciousness, but identify with each of the two in its own context.[140] If a people were to be interfered with or slaughtered before it had completed its mission, no other individual people would be able to take its place; peoples must live themselves out. Every nation is, in its karma, living through the things it has to live through in order to gain strength for its own task. Some nations may achieve their goal, while another with a different goal may not. Thereby something which only it could have achieved is lost, and instead it will adopt much that is not really suitable for it by imitating others. It is of great significance to pay attention to this.[141]

For this period we therefore need to consider the main national groupings separately.

Italy

The period of the Renaissance had looked back to classical times; so the progressive Folk Spirit at first remained in the spiritual world, selecting from there the characteristics it would require. Machiavelli (1506–27) then brought the politicizing of thoughts under the heathen forces from ancient Rome; and there was consequently a period of decline.[142]

Then, leading up to the middle of the sixteenth century, the Italian Folk Spirit descended through the sentient soul of its people. This particular Folk Spirit formed his physical body in air, warmth, light and sound, and his etheric body in life ether, burning desires, mobile susceptibility and wish substance (as described in the book *Theosophy* by Rudolf Steiner). This did not unify the politics, which remained in seven kingdoms (including the Papal States). But with the creation of the harpsichord in 1522, violin in 1530 and bassoon in 1539, Palestrina (1550–94) and Monteverdi (1592–1643) introduced a new impulse in music, the baroque repertoire, from which classical music and opera developed.[143]

For their contribution to science, however, Bruno was burned at the stake by the Inquisition in 1600 and Galileo (1589–1638), discoverer of the pendulum and exponent of the Copernican theory, was compelled to recant under threat of torture.

France

After the English left Calais in 1558, France—a mixture of Celtic and Frankish blood, Roman religion and culture—was self-contained. It was plunged at once into wars of religion (1562–98) between Catholics and the Calvinist Huguenots, who questioned the authority of both scripture and classics. After this awakening shock, the French Folk Spirit descended at the beginning of the seventeenth century through the intellectual soul of its people. The clever but immoral strategies of Richelieu (1616–42) and Mazarin (1643–57), which ignored religion, epitomized the intellectual-soul approach.[143]

France now saw it as her mission to create a fluent, lucid and exact language, and to unfold a great literature—Corneille (1636–50), Descartes (1637–64), Molière (1659–72) and Racine (1667–91) among them. Their thought sought to validate itself through its own strength: 'I think, therefore I am' (Descartes, but denied by every sleep). This was still a Greek type of culture, where people 'have thoughts' rather than 'think'.[144]

The unified state burst forth through Louis XIV (1651–1715), an absolute monarch who still claimed divine right: '*L'état, c'est moi.*' This led to the luciferic grandeur of the

Grand Siècle. French intellectuals saw themselves as leading the Age of Enlightenment, but the thoughts of Voltaire (1718–74) and Rousseau (1755–81) in fact derived from the abstract materialism of Locke and Hume in England. And whereas Diderot's 28-volume encyclopaedia aimed 'to transform the common way of thinking', it was economic problems which actually transformed people—and the freeing of serfs in 1780 was not enough.

The French Revolution (1784–94) arose with passionate impulsiveness, but the concepts of liberty, equality and fraternity were grasped abstractly, without regard for soul or spirit, and applied too ruthlessly. Here for the first time, however, instead of occult powers behind leading statesmen, people mostly spoke as people. But the attempt to emancipate the personality ended in the disastrous suppression of the personality.[145]

Napoleon (1795–1815), an enigmatic figure, stepped into the vacuum and tried to spread nationalism across Europe, dividing it among his family like an oriental potentate. His experiments were without a goal, and his attempts at colonization failed because their motivation was not economic but political. Meanwhile the wars guided by the English occult lodges through the two Pitts ruined France financially. When sea power was lost, Napoleon's urge to the East led him by land to Russia, where he failed again (1812), and his final defeat came at Waterloo in 1815.[146]

The relationship between the restored French monarchy and the Church remained abstract and unclear. People struggled to push back the Church but could not, because it dwelt in the depths of souls. Especially the Jesuit de Maistre (1796–1821) insisted on the sacred truth of the Fall, the godlessness and vapidity of the times, and the predestination of belonging either to the kingdom of God or that of this world. This view remained significant for more than a century.[147]

Britain

The English look back on the Elizabethan age (1558–1603) as an age of glory. It was a time of outward exploration and expansion. Wales had been incorporated in 1536. Through the defeat of the Armada in 1588 the forces of catholicism which resist the emancipation of the personality were warded off. The great all-human plays of Shakespeare (1592–1612) outshone many others—his characters live and act in the spiritual world due to his interest and sympathy for all around him. But Hamlet, the onlooker, doubts the spirit, which appears to him as a ghost (spiritual materialism), and inwardly he is confused and uncertain—this is the characteristic of the British soul. There were, however, poetry and music, and historians who studied the human mind; and the free creation of thoughts in the consciousness soul was beginning. There was a brief renaissance impulse around Prince Henry (1609–12), drawing on Florence and those around John Dee (1551–1608), which advanced the arts, science and invention. Even Newton (1571–1630) was aware of spiritual realities behind the stars.[148]

When James VI and I united the crowns of Scotland and England in 1603 (political union was not until 1707), he brought with him old traditions from the sentient-soul age carried by lodges of Freemasonry behind the Scottish clan system. Catholic opposition resulted in the gunpowder plot of 1605. James, however, felt the religion of his age to be a masquerade, and his personality did not fit English life, where everyone wanted to be a 'king'. He spread the seeds for a network of Masonic lodges in the principal cities of Europe. But sign, grip and cultic word work compulsively into the etheric body, preventing that free understanding which is the moral basis of the consciousness soul. This was further anaesthetized by admitting only aristocracy and gentry, even to so-called 'operative' lodges. Though these were outwardly innocuous, the central lodge (from 1717 the

Grand Lodge) gained great influence. The object of those who directed the British state was to dominate Graeco–Latin (French–Spanish) culture, by dividing it into separate groups and orders, but especially by spreading nationalism. Edinburgh Masons sang in 1638 'For we be brethren of the Rosy Cross, we have the Mason's word and second sight'. But the real Rosicrucian impulse lay rather with Robert Fludd (1616–37).[149]

The inductive thinking set out in the *Novum Organum* (1620) of Francis Bacon, who regarded concepts as 'idols' unless derived from the observation of many sense-phenomena, coupled with the educational methods of Comenius (1631–59), drew intellectuals further into the sense world. Characteristically Cherbury, with no real experience of Christ, asked in 1624 whether it is 'reasonable' to believe in Christ? In contrast, puritanism drew the populace away from reality through belief in an entirely abstract Old Testament (moon) God disconnected from the sense-world. This was the time of the *Mayflower* (1620) and the puritan exodus to America. After the Civil War between Royalists and Parliament, and the execution of the self-isolated Charles I in 1649, government came into the hands of the puritan Oliver Cromwell (1643–58) as head of the Commonwealth. In the middle of the century, while aristocracy had temporarily lost control, the English Folk Spirit descended into the consciousness soul (which is based on the physical body). British political institutions now became the most advanced and free. Even after the Restoration in 1660 kingship was a shadow no longer alive here.[150]

From 1640 to 1660 Rosicrucian Hermeticists around Thomas Vaughan were seeking a thorough reform of society, education and religion. Protestantism in Britain would have nothing to do with the medieval abstractions of an analytical form of wisdom such as Scholasticism; the faith for which it fought was a last relic of 'life without knowledge' (p. 41). This turning away from the thinking spirit simply perpetuated the disastrous effects of the dogma of 869. It was led by a backward Archon working as Archangel. The Baptists, founded in 1609, practised total immersion, and were distantly related to the Albigenses. The Society of Friends or Quakers, founded by George Fox in 1652, depended on guidance from Christ through the inner life and on study of the Bible, with no ritual or ministers—much like the original Celtic Church. In response to the Hermeticists, the Royal Society was founded in 1662 as a bastion of materialism alongside Anglicanism and Freemasonry.[151]

The very influential philosophy of Locke (1689–93) was in keeping with the ahrimanic initiation of the Scottish lodges. He said that objects have only substance, shape and movement, and that these momentarily produce in the senses colour, tone and so on, which can be thought about but do not exist. He faced events as an onlooker, with the soul no more than a blank sheet; the ego described by the German philosophers he altogether ignored, and all higher reality was excluded. For Berkeley (1710) sense-data exist, but he knew nothing of material objects—only of spirits working on one another. More significant, though unfortunately of little influence, was the view of Shaftesbury (1711): percepts enter the soul through the outer senses, thoughts through the 'inner sense'; beauty and truth are shadows of a higher reality. For Hume (1742–57) experience is governed only by mental habit, not by any real world. His scepticism was a major influence on the Continent, especially on those who inspired the French Revolution, and on Kant.[152]

The combination of the developing science and technology with the Anglo-Saxon impulse towards economic life set up the individuality and made England a major commercial power. And the disposition in those who by nature speak English—a language strong in words for outer phenomena—to cultivate the consciousness soul, to connect intelligence with world events, brought the expansion of empire. Despite the War of Independence, trade with America was still dominant, and the founding of the Bank of England in 1694 and new inventions spurred the Industrial Revolution which started in 1770. There was a climate of freedom to which Burke (1769–90) brought a sober liberalism, with economic reforms based on a concept of nations as organisms, which benefited mankind in general. The Whigs continued this concern, though deeply modified in practice by the view of Adam Smith (1776) that economic life depends on individual self-interest and the profit motive, a view which still prevails. The Tories (backed by the Lodges) still saw themselves in contrast as patriarchal landowners with their vassals (which harked back to Homeric Greece). The death sentence for theft or poaching lasted until the 1820s, and child labour until 1833. During this century Freemasonry incorporated the new business and industrial classes, bringing them to the ways of the gentry, but thereby retarding economic development and such things as education and women's liberation. The British were now truly 'the people of the Lodges'.[153]

Germanic Countries

There was still in the sixteenth century a feeling for elemental beings. Paracelsus (1500–26) and Tycho Brahe (1577–1601) were both aware of spiritual realities behind nature, though this was a culture of the few. The Rosicrucian brotherhood (p. 63) flourished most strongly in Central Europe, and received a new impulse when the young Valentin Andreae was inspired by a spiritual power not then in incarnation to pen the imagination of the *Chymical Wedding* in 1604. This was followed by the *Fama* and the *Confession*. This movement tried to heal the rift between mankind and the world of spirit caused by materialistic thinking, by uniting a freshly experienced Christianity with both art and a spiritualized natural science.[154]

But this great Germanic spiritual impulse was virtually annihilated by the disastrous Thirty Years War (1618–48), in which a third of the German population was lost. The protestant culture of Central Europe was assaulted by the Counter-Reformation, led by the luciferic forces of Jesuitism and the Habsburgs, while James I refused to help. Outwardly nothing was changed, but inwardly souls were diverted from the spirit, developing spiritual organs were paralysed, and the Rosicrucian social impulse was frustrated. In 1698 the vast Habsburg Empire reverted to its various parts.[155]

In the Netherlands the Protestant spirit had already confronted catholicism, though it was refusal to pay Spanish taxes that led to independence for the United Provinces in 1579. The Spirit of the Age needed an instrument to extend the influence of Europe to, for example, the East Indies (1595–1620). This brought a vast increase in shipping, and hence in investment, by 1670. Later a Folk Spirit and Language Spirit conjoined, changing the Dutch temperament. This was the age of the great Dutch painters, with their eyes set firmly on sense reality: Van Dyck (1617–39), Rembrandt (1632–69), Vermeer (1656–69). Rembrandt's paintings show the rise of the Protestant spirit against Catholicism. Spinoza (1675) experienced the ego as a divine substance which thinks and acts.[156]

We may sense the mood of great profundity and warmth in Central Europe through the great musicians: Bach (1717–49), Haydn (1764–98), Mozart (1770–91), Beethoven (1792–1825), Schubert (1813–28). Most unusually, many Central Europeans had been incarnated there before as members of the Germanic tribes, and these tended to confront one another rather than unite—hence the 300 petty courts. In 1750 there were 50 universities among them (in England, two!). Under Frederick the Great (1740–86) Prussia emerged as predominant, while Austria had the powerful rule of Maria Theresa (1740–80). Napoleon then in 1806 assembled 16 princes of the largest kingdoms to form the German Reich.[157]

But this is above all the time of the great German thinkers. Lessing (1776–81), with his concept of reincarnation, experienced the ego as rooted in a world of spiritual reality extending beyond the sense world. Kant (1781–90) placed the whole experience of nature into the mind; if there is a thing-in-itself it can never be known. Schiller (1781–1805) found the realm of freedom and art between the sense world and the necessity of reason. Goethe (1769–1812) placed the human spirit out in the natural world, and experienced beauty and art as a higher stage at which the laws of nature speak of themselves within man. He brought a living thinking—that is, a Christianized, resurrected thinking—to grasp the archetypes of living organisms. Fichte (1793–1807) said: I am, and I attribute existence to the world; but what I do participates in a moral world order, a supersensible world, independent of myself. Schelling (1793–1815) filled his ego with mental pictures created by nature, and felt nature as identical with what in us is intelligence and consciousness. Nature is thus spiritualized into laws, with no trace of matter. The cosmic spirit remembers its deeds in my knowing, and repeats them in miniature in artistic creating. Hegel (1807–21) saw the highest human activity in thinking which becomes conscious of itself. Thought is the essence of all things, and through it the soul lives the life of the world spirit as its own life. Thus all these men except Kant bring a new spiritual substance, a new experience of realism, which could indeed then be grasped only by a few, yet (without any state structure) laid the foundation for a spiritual Central Europe, and for the future Sixth Epoch.[158]

Into the ego that the philosophers were describing, the Germanic Folk Spirit had descended around 1750. In 1828 appeared in Baden the tragic figure of Casper Hauser, destined to bring this spiritual culture to full fruition. But he was forcibly prevented in a repulsive manner from doing so by British occultism (through Lord Stanhope), to the great loss not only of Germany but of the whole of Europe. Instead, the way was opened for Prussian domination. Between 1830 and 1850 the Germanic Folk Spirit withdrew again, acting only on the soul element and leaving the ego to develop on its own in the physical world. But this leaves the ego open to the opposing powers if it fails to rise to the spiritual world where the guidance of the Folk Spirit is henceforth to be found. Contemplation of the true 'I' thus vanished with the idealistic philosophy of Central Europe in the middle of the nineteenth century. Again the developing spirituality was frustrated. From this flowed the future destiny of Germany.[159]

Slav Countries

By the sixteenth century Moscow had become absolute, with a wealthy Church and its own patriarch. Icons, produced since 1300, and fine frescoes and illuminations, were still being made. When Ivan the Terrible (1533–84) named himself Tsar, claiming both temporal and spiritual leadership, he drew on a western concept 'Christ is King and the Tsar his representative', which was foreign to the mood of 'Holy Russia' to the effect that 'Christ is Spirit'. The peasantry responded to his rule of terrorism and the annihilation of the whole boyar nobility by mass migrations to the periphery.[160]

The new regent, Boris Godunov (1584–1605) tried to bring in western influences and forces of the intellectual soul. But after he murdered the heir—8½-year-old Dmitri, a soul of great importance comparable for Russia to Casper Hauser—catastrophes led to the unnatural deaths of himself and his son. Immediately a 'false Dmitri' trained by Jesuits in Poland was put forward with the Pope's blessing, under whom the Uniate Church was founded, with Eastern liturgy yet subservient to the Pope and Catholic dogmas. But he was so indifferent to Russian ways that he too was killed in an insurrection. Jesuit/Polish efforts to dominate continued, but the first of the Romanovs was chosen in 1613 and ruled with understanding.

Peter I (1689–1725) tried to destroy Russia's history and spiritual past to make way for western ideas. He mocked Christianity, subjugated the Church and abolished confession. Mistranslations in the Bible were corrected, but what remained of the esoteric cult was at the same time destroyed. Hence the 'Old Believers' saw him as a demon and rebelled, over 20,000 including whole villages being burned to death (1672–91). After visiting Holland and Britain and becoming a Mason, Peter established a huge army, navy and armaments industry, paid for by punitive taxation and serfdom. He not only built St Petersburg, at great cost of life, but instituted a secret police, split the nobility and intelligentsia from the populace, and placed the idea of the state above conscience and morality. The forces of the intellectual soul were thus misused ahrimanically. Through all this the peasantry remained true to their inner nature.[161]

The spurious 'Testament of Peter' created conditions already planned by western occulists, under which the Anglo-Saxon world was to be the 'guardian' of Eastern Europe, and Central Europe was to be destroyed. This influenced Russian foreign policy until the twentieth century. During the reigns of Catherine the Great and Paul (1762–1825) a German system of administration and medical and cultural reforms were introduced. An influx of Jesuits (temporarily banned elsewhere) inhibited the work of the Rosicrucians, but their influence as well as those of western occultism in politics and literature continued. De

Maistre (1810–21) brought a strong influence from the Roman Church, presenting the papacy as the rightful ruler of modern civilization.[162]

Polish initiative drove the Turks back from Hungary (1683–1717) but the Balkans remained under their yoke, though Bosnia was freed in 1717. Poland itself was then partitioned between Prussia, Austria and Russia (1772–95), and was re-established as a part of Russia in 1815. Its subsequent Russification provoked strong forces of individuality there.

The Russian Folk Spirit, whose lowest principle is that of light and his others two degrees above those of Italy, extending to the realm of Soul Light (the Mercury-sphere), has not yet been ready to descend to his people.[163]

Spiritual Reality and Dead Thinking

The supersensible School of Michael (p. 66) had already ended soon after the eighteenth century began. But during the first half of the nineteenth century Michael conducted a cosmic cult in the spiritual world to prepare his followers through mighty imaginations for his future regency. Goethe gave an indication of this in his tale of 'The Green Snake and the Beautiful Lily' (translated by Carlyle). Then at the start of the 1840s Michael took up his task as Spirit of the Age for the fifth post-Atlantean epoch (lasting to about AD 3500) and rose to the rank of Archai (Time Spirits or Spirits of Personality). With this is connected the descent of the Archangel Michael from the sun into our earth region. Then between 1842 and 1879 Michael undertook the battle which brought about the fall of the Spirits of Darkness, the dragon forces, from heaven into mankind on earth. Mankind thus became liable to temptation from new forces of evil, but is strengthened by Michael to withstand them with new powers of perception and will.[164]

Now since Lemuria, when the Fullness of the seven Elohim had created man in their own image, one of them, Jehovah, separated himself from sun to moon, bestowing wisdom on humanity but excluding the forces of the other six Elohim from human evolution—thereby creating lower spiritual entities who were antisocial. But in the 1840s Jehovah could no longer master these opposing spirits, who acquired such power that no social impulse was wholesome without an understanding of the Christ-impulse.[165]

By the early 1840s certain retarded Angels had also tried to supplant the Archangels in the human nervous system, making people so clever that they could enter public life in their twenties. At the same time, thinking in the consciousness soul, which is itself a transformation by the ego of forces freed from the physical body, fell back on the physical body and the forces of death. For the vast majority of people it became a shadowy, subjective corpse which reached a culmination of abstractedness and emptiness. Faith in the human mind, such as that of the German thinkers, was lost. Instead, everything was made to depend on usefulness or profit.[166]

The many materialistic souls now rising after death into the etheric world brought there a new human darkness. In that world Christ dwelt in the form of an Angel (as He once took the physical form of man), and for Him this darkness amounted to a second crucifixion. If one seeks from an historical and psychological point of view truly to understand the origin of this new materialism, one must seek it in the Roman Church. It was the Church which in 869 had denied the reality of spirit, after which religious faith was filled only with old oriental traditions from a previous age. Then in 1854 was promulgated under Jesuit influence the dogma of the immaculate conception, a physical travesty of the conception of the cosmic Sophia in the purified soul of Mary. There followed an encyclical declaring all freedom of conscience and religious practice as a mark of delirium or madness. Finally in 1870, a thousand years after the denial of the spirit, the infallibility of the papal office, which has no support in scripture, was pronounced to the faithful. The early Church Fathers would have called it blasphemy. Thus was the living experience of Christ, who remains with us to the end of the earth, denied.[167]

Especially in the Anglo-Saxon area, any search for the divine through philosophy or meditation was now replaced by an atheistic natural science, whose consciousness is so dimmed that it has to receive direction from the observation of experiments instead of through thinking. But this can only reach the corpse of reality. Darwin considered only body and soul, ignoring the spirit. And it is characteristic that his theory of the struggle for existence and the survival of the fittest not only dominated natural science (1859), but also, through writers such as Spencer (1857–70), increasingly poisoned the social sciences with notions of superior and inferior races, peoples and customs. Meanwhile Goethe's insights into metamorphosis (1787) and Kropotkin's view of survival through mutual help (1904) were ignored. For the universities are the greatest impediment to new, living thinking in the consciousness soul. Their doubts about thinking found classic expression in the assertion of 'limits of knowledge' by Du Bois Reymond (1872–80).[168]

As regards the soul, science had nothing but words jingling around, and even tried to experiment with souls as if they were objects of nature, instead of deepening the inner experience. Nevertheless, science did provide a counterpoise to abstract theology. Insistence on the supposedly inviolable 'law' of conservation of energy, for example, matches the dogma of papal infallibility—both exclude the free ascent to spiritual experience.[169]

Now that commerce was expanding to a world economy, such dead thinking could not comprehend that either. It was left to develop according to instincts from the past, causing widespread misery. The Free Trade movement in

English liberalism led by Cobden and Bright (1846–60), who were schooled in self-discipline and overcame nationalism, could if taken further have been of greatest significance. But the middle classes were totally sterile of ideas and the Lodges, who then saw any idea of a united Europe as a threat, prevented it.[170]

The death forces of the intellect were also carried into social life. The result in proletarian consciousness was socialism, which is latent not in the soul but in the temperament. Consciences were stirred through a new moral indignation at inhumanity and injustice amidst increasing industrialism. Search was made for an idea of society in which individual freedom could have its place, but the shadowy intellect could not find this; for socialism cannot succeed without the spirit, and there was no confidence in spirit. Marx and Engels (1848–67) were also the direct outcome of the denial of the spirit in 869, but carried this further in their far-reaching attempts to abolish the soul and recognize only the struggle for material well-being. The proletariat were thus thrust into the realm of the machine. Karl Marx, having observed the crucial nature of economics, the surplus value created by work but taken by management, and the need for workers to struggle, set out to reform on the basis of hatred, organizing class instincts like a general his troops. Socialism is destined to develop, but it first works like a religion, with great intolerance. At least in Britain and France slavery was abolished, strikes were legalized, trade unions were recognized and socialist MPs elected (1815–64).[171]

The western occult brotherhoods of course knew of the spiritual and elemental worlds, and some members did wish that the latter and the working of social forces should be made public through mediumship. Others wished to misuse mediumship for their particular political ends, especially to exclude any knowledge of reincarnation. The former prevailed, but when mediums spoke allegedly but mistakenly about the deceased it was all hushed up. One result, greater than one would think, was a super-materialism in the sense of Locke.[172]

Thus in this period the old ideas had finally become emptied of reality, and nationalistic materialism took root. Spirituality was driven back everywhere. But the truth is that it is just through reacting against a mechanistic culture filled with death forces that individuals can develop the spiritual soul. That is why it is necessary for mankind to experience the degeneration of the environment at the present time. And that is just what the western Lodges wish to conceal.[173]

Europe

A parliament of Europe, to arbitrate between nations and impose its awards, was proposed by Penn in 1693, but not taken up. After the aggrandisement of Napoleon, dreams of a united Europe arose again. In 1815 Talleyrand and Metternich formed a 'Concert of Europe' from Britain, France, Austria, Prussia and Russia, but it was very backward-looking; Britain withdrew in 1820, and it collapsed. A further attempt without Britain was even more retrograde, seeking to suppress the modern consciousness emerging.[174]

Between 1815 and 1830 Switzerland, Greece and Belgium became independent. Then under Bismarck (1859–90) Prussia expanded through the Austro-Prussian War of 1866 and took Alsace-Lorraine in 1870, arousing lasting hatred in France. In 1871 the German nation was united under Prussia (though remaining differentiated in thought and language). Thereby the true task of Central Europe, as expressed in the great German thinkers, was excluded. After the Pope had condemned 'progress, liberalism and civilization as lately introduced', Bismarck expelled the Jesuits, imprisoned bishops, and introduced civil marriages.[175]

A similar union of states took place in Italy (1860–70) through Cavour and Garibaldi. The dynamic forces of Catholic fervour had now turned against catholicism in favour of nationalism. In the Balkans, Romania (1856–59) and Bulgaria (1878) also became independent. Russia defeated Turkey (1878), and Britain and Austro-Hungary intervened both to give Serbia and Montenegro independence and to promise Bosnia to Austro-Hungary—two problem areas in 1914.[176]

In Russia itself the collapse of the Magyar rising (1849) was followed by the Crimean War (1854–56), in which western Lodges in Britain and France, allied with the decadent Turkey, first attacked the People of Christ. In 1864 serfs were at last freed in Russia, though they were little better off. But the Tsar was murdered by anarchists just before signing more reforms in 1881.

8
THE PRESENT SUN REGENCY OF MICHAEL—THE BATTLE FOR THE SPIRIT
From 1879 to the twenty-second century

Michael

To recapitulate, Michael was in ancient times the Sun Archangel, leader of the planetary Archangels, and Ruler of the Cosmic Intelligence. He was (and is) one of the four Archangels of the year. He was also at first the Countenance of Jehovah, his representative to the Hebrew people. From about 550 to 200 BC he took precedence in sequence as the Archangel of Time of Classical Greece, his influence ending soon after the Mystery of Golgotha.[177]

Around that time he ceased to be the Countenance of Jehovah and became instead the Countenance of Christ. From the fourth century the Cosmic Intelligence fell from his grasp to humanity on earth. And in the ninth century the other planetary Archangels rebelled against his leadership. At some time during this period Michael, who 'went in front of the Christ-impulse', became one of the many Germanic Archangels. After receiving teaching from a kind of Roman Spirit of the Age and uniting with the Spirit of Exoteric Christianity from the twelfth to the sixteenth century, he took precedence among them. But from the fifteenth to the beginning of the eighteenth century he was directing his Supersensible School in the spiritual world, while the other Germanic Archangels each went his own way, many serving the Spirit of Exoteric Christianity directly.[178]

During the sixteenth to seventeenth centuries Michael was further prepared in compromise with the Egyptian Spirit of the Age, recently a Spirit of Form. About 1750 the German Folk Spirit (presumably then Michael) descended into his people, but about 1830 he rose again to the soul world. During the first half of the nineteenth century Michael was conducting his Cosmic Cult in the spiritual world.[179]

Then in 1841 Michael rose to the rank of Archon and took up his task as Spirit of the Fifth Age. Between 1842 and 1879 he drove the Spirits of Darkness from heaven into mankind on earth. In 1879 he then took over also as ruling Time Archangel, working in harmony with the newly appointed Germanic Archangel to bring the Christ-impulse to expression. He alone of the Planetary Archangels still seeks to co-ordinate the forces of the cosmos for the benefit of mankind.[180]

His impulse now is to lead mankind once more to read in the book of nature, to recognize the supersensible in the immediate sense world, the spiritual in the material, and thus to rescue thinking from the mechanistic rule of Ahriman. He works for all those who seek the paths to spiritual science. He seeks to establish his citadel in human heads so that understanding of Christ as Sun Being may arise again. Our task is to find living ideas, living concepts, living feelings in place of dead theories—and this comes directly from the beings united with Michael.[181]

Michael is the spirit of strength who enables us to do this. His impulse of cosmopolitanism, for example, leads to the overcoming of nationalism, racism and ethnic conflict. He brings also the power through which human karma (disordered by the influences of Archangels opposing) him can be brought back into order. The image of him is so strong in us that to devote our feelings to him depends only on our good will to feel the dragon who drags us down, and to see his luminous being vanquish it. Michael the Warrior, defending the Cosmic Spirit against the ahrimanic powers under his feet, inspires mankind with his own being, and the leading of civilization out of decline is bound up with our understanding of him.[182]

The Dawn of Light

As the result of the fall of the Spirits of Darkness a new light shone in the heavens for those who could look upwards, although a new darkness enveloped others—whether they knew it or not. This was, for example, the golden age of Russian literature, with Gorki (1882–1910), Tolstoy (1865–99) and Chekhov (1896–1904). In Solovieff (1878–1900) the inspiration of Christ was so powerful that he felt every action, right down to the muscles, to be permeated by Him, and in his concern for questions of evil, suffering and death he could not imagine social life not ordained by Christ. This is a counter-impulse to the atavistic clairvoyance and will of Jesuitism. Alongside a few such intellectuals, the masses in Russia were still sleeping deep in Orthodoxy.[183]

The Theosophical Society was founded in 1875 by Blavatsky (1875–89), the most competent modern exponent of ancient mediumship and clairvoyance. An Esoteric School was founded within the Society in 1888. Sinnett, however, (1884) gave a materialistic view of spiritual matters.[184]

But it was Rudolf Steiner (1882–1925) who gave the new insight clear thought form. As a boy he lived closely with the elemental world; from the age of 8 he had visions of the soul world; and during his adolescence he struggled with the nature of the 'I'. In editing Goethe's work on metamorphosis his capacity for Imagination unfolded, and his editorial work in Weimar (1890–96) required him to enter with Inspiration into those around him. His *Philosophy of Freedom* (1894) completed philosophy by re-establishing thought as part of reality (realism) and the thinking ego as able to act in freedom. Thereby the Arthurian experience of the cosmos and the inner Grail experience were united as two pillars that bear certainty regarding the spiritual world. Through Intuition he stood in 1899 before the Mystery of Golgotha in 'most inward, most earnest joy of knowledge.'[185]

This year 1899 brought the end of 5000 years of the Dark Age (Kali Yuga). Not only did all the beings of the spiritual world have to co-operate in this but the initiates had quietly to prepare people for it. Now mankind as a whole began to live across the threshold of the spiritual world, in hell as well as heaven, though this was not yet recognized. Moreover, beings from the realm of Vulcan were entering evolution for the first time, who not only brought messages of a comprehensive spiritual science but wanted it willed into social action.[186]

The new age ushered in the first phase of Anthroposophy (1902–09), a wisdom based on knowledge of the relationship between macrocosm and microcosm, in which Steiner was inspired by the Maitreya Bodhisattva, a being of angelic standing. The second phase of Anthroposophy (1909–16) began with insights into the Gospels suggesting that Steiner was now inspired directly by Jesus of Nazareth, an Archangel being. He revealed a quite new possibility to perceive the approach of Christ in the form of an Angel in the etheric world, as a brother to those in distress. Through union with the macrocosm and its objective creative forces, Steiner was able to give a unique impulse to the renewal of the arts, including the Mystery Dramas (1910–13), the creation of Eurythmy, and the building of the Goetheanum (1913–18).[187]

The Onslaught of Darkness

From the outset of the Michael age we can recognize the increasing adverse activity from the Archangels opposing him: Gabriel's moon forces (reaching back to the third age, that of Jehovah) in the occultism of the western brotherhoods; Samael's Mars forces in the aggressiveness of the times; Raphael's Mercury forces in the transcendentalism of the Churches rooted in the fourth age; Zachariel's Jupiter forces in the abstract intellectualism of scientific and popular thinking; Anael's Venus forces in the egoism crying out for transformation into love, and in the sensualism of much modern art; and Oriphiel's Saturn forces in Roman legalism and bureaucracy.

The western Lodges inspired by Ahriman have had three goals: to suppress the luciferic forces from the fourth epoch centred in the Catholic Church and the states supporting it; to ensure that humanity does not advance beyond the consciousness-soul development of the fifth epoch; and to undermine and enslave the Slavic and especially the Russian people, who bear the seed forces for the incorporation of Spirit Self in the sixth epoch. To this end they sought to spread materialism through Anglo-American world domination, and to suppress the spiritual forces of the ego which repeatedly arose as the hallmark of German-speaking culture, currently in the form of Anthroposophy (which the forces of catholicism equally seek to suppress).

They consequently sought to transform Europe from the Rhine to the Urals into economic slaves. In the 1880s they circulated a map showing a Danube–Balkan union, a Slav confederation, and the coast from Holland to Italy 'under English influence'. The Russian state was to disappear, so that socialist experiments might be undertaken there whose aim was to turn the people away from Christianity, to sap their energies, and to practise totalitarian control for application elsewhere.[188]

In 1882 Bismarck, fearing French retribution for having taken Alsace-Lorraine, had formed a defensive triple alliance with Austria and Italy—an unusual step in peace time. Germany had tried to emulate the French, and the French hated what they saw of themselves; and the English hated them for taking up science and industry, the basis of English prosperity. British secret diplomacy was preparing war against Germany from at least 1877, and used the Vatican to bring about a *rapprochement* between France and Russia, which led to the dual alliance of 1894, the first step towards encircling Central Europe—which it had long feared (see p. 55). Especially after Bismarck's fall in 1890, Germany turned its back on its true spiritual heritage from the days of Goethe, and took up enthusiastically British social Darwinism, with grandiose dreams of world empire. Such national egoism played into the hands of the occult forces stirring fear of Germany among the masses, and from 1901 the British press stirred antagonism against Germany.[189]

By 1904 Britain and France had formed the *Entente Cordiale*, an informal commitment sponsored by Edward VII (then Masonic Grand Protector). In 1906 Admiral Fisher accurately predicted that war with Germany would start in 1914, and an arms race began. From this time the Upper House was reduced to a virtual shadow. The following year Britain and Russia, for long enemies, also came to agreement. The Tsar's anti-Semitic policies had meanwhile sparked pogroms (1903), which caused large-scale Jewish emigration, and ultimately gave rise to Zionism and the return to Palestine (1917).

Meanwhile consciousness of the disintegrating earth entered artistic life. French Impressionism brought a freshness and intensification of perception to visual art, but its technique based on minute particles of colour did not live on. The new consciousness was clearly visible in Picasso (1900–50), Kandinsky (1910–34) and the Expressionists. It was also evident in the expressionistic pantonal and later twelve-tone music of Schoenberg (1899–1936) and his pupils. In the intellectual life Freud (1899–1930) began his work on dream-interpretation based on sexuality, from which psychoanalysis developed. Einstein evolved his abstract Theory of Relativity (1905). Whitehead and Russell in their *Principia Mathematica* (1910–13) derived the whole of mathematics and logic from five simple concepts drawn from nowhere. And theology concentrated on 'Jesus the Man'. High Church, however, knew more occultism than the Theosophical Society, and sought to eliminate any understanding by others of reincarnation and of man's participation in the cosmos.[190]

Socialism continued to gain strength, and Labour and Social Democratic parties were formed. But economic and social impulses were not informed by an understanding of the spirit. The threat of revolution moved Russia towards constitutional monarchy, but the representation of peasants and workers was unjust, so terrorism and repression continued there. The Russification of Ukraine, Poland and the Baltic peoples and the persecution of the Jews intensified.

By 1913 the Balkans were freed from the Turks. Crown Prince Franz Ferdinand of Austria (1896–1914) tried to give the empire's Slavs self-government in a peaceful triad with Austria and Hungary, but Serbia agitated to take Bosnia from it. Bulgaria then attacked Serbia, with the support of both Russia—aiming for the Dardanelles—and western occultism. Next, terrorists associated with the Black Hand, a Serbian secret society with government connections, murdered Franz Ferdinand and his Slav wife while on an official visit to Sarajevo. To punish Serbia, Austria issued a harsh ultimatum followed by declaration of war. Germany would have left them to it, but a snare of rigid treaties (including a secret commitment to France by Grey, kept even from the British cabinet from 1905 to 1911), rigid military plans and a lowered consciousness in responsible circles extended it to the First World War, as English occultism had planned—though either Grey or the Russians could easily have prevented it.[191]

The Russian Revolution of 1917 was started by middle-class Menscheviks, but they lacked ideas. At the treaty of

Brest-Litovsk with Russia (1918) the German Foreign Minister had promised to introduce Steiner's 'Memorandum' on the separation of spiritual and economic life from political control, which could have been done in Russia, but he did not. Instead the 'social experiment' planned by western occultism enabled the proletarian Bolsheviks, with secret American finance, to step in. Lenin (1918–24) was brought in and at first acted like a tsar, central control was undiminished, and there was no real change. Then in the Bolshevik revolution and the civil war between Reds and Whites (supported by western allies) a chaotic interplay arose between backward spiritual forces of Central Asia and Siberia that had remained from Atlantean times, and modern forces from the West. The economy collapsed, scores of thousands were executed, and hundreds of thousands sent to concentration camps (1918–20). Famine in 1921 led to a free market for peasant products, but only briefly. Lenin's policy of 'collectivization' destroyed the unique village communities developed centuries before on a truly social basis, thereby destroying the peasant's connection with the land, which had always reflected for him not only the sunlight but also the spirit within it.[192]

After the defeat of Germany and eight and a half million dead, the peace treaty—brokered by an outsider, the American Woodrow Wilson, who lived in idealistic abstractions—was signed five years to the day since the assassination at Sarajevo. This broke Austria/Hungary into six parts on the basis of spurious linguistic nationalism, invented Czechoslovakia and Yugoslavia, and thwarted its role in harmonizing Central Europe. Under punitive reparations the German mark collapsed in 1923, because the state tried to run the economy against the financial markets; those with property and debts suffered little, while savers lost everything. The Balkan democracies then failed, due to economic problems and dissatisfied minorities. Here the Roman image of man as a purely physical entity worked like a spectre, and the unjust consequences engendered hatred.

The old Europe built on old ideas was by now illusion; everything built up since the first Christian centuries—including Christianity as so far presented by the Churches—was irreparably smashed (but this was not perceived). People subconsciously demanded something new, which the conservative forces repressed. When a stream is blocked, rapids appear; the rapids of European culture had been reached.[193]

New Impulses Suppressed

Rudolf Steiner, now directly inspired by Michael as Archon, Spirit of the Age, stood virtually alone against the decline of civilization. His proposal for healing social life through the movement for Threefold Ordering—freedom of the individual spirit, equality of rights within a group, brotherhood and association in a world economy, each separately organized yet integrated—was everywhere rejected. Other occult groups opposed freedom of the spirit as inimical to their own power, even to the extent of attacks on his life in 1922 and 1923, and arson of the Goetheanum building. Instead, theories of science (apart from actual facts) were shaped into materialistic pictures of atoms, molecules, neutrons and the like, small 'demons' which cannot be experienced and hold individuals in occult imprisonment. To reach the spirit today it is necessary instead to go through the human organism. Nevertheless the anthroposophical educational movement, curative education, the medical movement, biodynamic agriculture, artistic and scientific work were all placed on a sound if small foundation, as well as the movement for religious renewal founded by Dr Rittelmeyer. The Christmas Foundation meeting of the Anthroposophical Society and the founding of the School of Spiritual Science (1923) formed the culmination of Steiner's work.[194]

During the widespread depression of 1929–33, the Briand plan proposed a federal link between the countries of Europe (1930) and introduced ideas of 'European Community' and 'common market', but this was rejected by the larger countries. They paid lip-service to Wilson's League of Nations, founded without America in 1919, which lacked power, never achieved results, and collapsed in 1934, although serving as a prototype for later.

In 1933 a spiritual event of outstanding importance occurred, though experienced at first by very few people. This was the appearance of Christ in the etheric world, which may be seen as a second resurrection, and will grow over the next two and a half millennia into a mighty force. This 'appearing' in the etheric (1 Timothy 6:14) is the second of four stages, of which the first was the physical incarnation in the Jewish people culminating in the Mystery of Golgotha, the third will be His 'revelation' in an astral body in the Russian culture of the sixth epoch (2 Thessalonians 1:7), and the last will be the actual Second Coming (Parousia) as Cosmic Ego in the seventh post-Atlantean epoch (Matthew 24:3–37). Since Christ is the true higher Ego of all humanity, this event is significant for the whole of mankind, but occurs first among the Germanic peoples, who have been most awake to experiences of the inner life.[195]

But the greatest light appears in the greatest darkness, and in opposition to the appearance of the Etheric Christ the Beast of the Apocalypse, who attacks the ego directly, arose from the abyss of unconsciousness alongside Lucifer and Ahriman. For it was in 1933 also that Hitler became Chancellor of Germany (the heart of Europe), and began the extermination first of six million Jews (people of the fourth epoch) and later of 20 million Russians (people of the sixth epoch). The Germans were uniquely vulnerable to forces of darkness because their Folk Spirit had withdrawn, and guides only those who rise to the spiritual world. Hitler began at once with the concentration camps and suppression of the Catholic and Social Democratic Parties (1933), the 'Night of the Long Knives', and the occupation of the demilitarized Rhineland (1934)—significantly without opposition from France or Britain. Nazi propaganda was so logical that most people did not perceive its destructive will, until the occupation of Austria in 1938 and of Poland and Czechoslovakia in 1939 brought about the Second World War. The Holocaust of the Jews began in January 1942.[196]

In Russia, Stalin (1922–53) also began his purges in 1934 that wiped out 15 million people; and through industrialization and the 'cultural revolution' (lasting to the 1950s) the remainder were subjected to an indoctrination that sought to implant a thoroughly ahrimanic consciousness soul. Meanwhile, in Italy, Mussolini (1919–45) was developing Fascist nationalism, and Franco (1936–75) began his civil war with the Spanish royalists. Totalitarianism thus led the concept of nation-state to absurd excess.[197]

By 1942 Hitler controlled a region similar in size to Charlemagne and Napoleon, but, as in the case of the latter, his invasion of Russia failed. The turning-point came in 1943 at Stalingrad, El Alamein and Guadalcanal, after American intervention in 1941. But Allied claims to morality were compromised by the carpet-bombing of Germany and the ultimate terror of the atom bomb. Even before the liberation of the West, three old men—Roosevelt, Churchill and Stalin—felt competent to redraw the map of Europe without consulting the peoples concerned and without any new ideas. By the end of the War in 1945 the destruction of Central Europe and the partition of Germany—long planned by the western brotherhoods—were achieved. And through all these events in the twelve years from 1933 to 1945 experience of the Etheric Christ was almost entirely obscured.

In 1947 the Opus Dei, a secretive Catholic lay organization (1920), was recognized by Rome. It rests on mortification of the body, vows of poverty and chastity, and absolute obedience even in details of daily life and work (i.e. the suppression of the ego). It claims that truth is fully revealed for ever, so that anything new is not from God. It aims to dominate the professions, especially university teaching, and claims to serve Raphael, Gabriel and Michael. Other Catholics criticize it as dangerous, loveless and unchristian.

The Cold War

The tension between capitalism and communism, America and the Soviet Union, was reflected in the division of Germany into the Federal and Democratic Republics in 1949. Europe was forced to cower between America, which had used the atomic bomb against Japan in 1945, and Russia, which acquired it in 1949 (succeeded by the hydrogen bomb in 1952). The Campaign for Nuclear Disarmament was launched in 1958, 33 years after Steiner's death.

As intended since before 1941, America dominated world government, setting up the United Nations and International Monetary Fund in 1945, the World Bank in 1946, and the General Agreement on Tariffs and Trade in 1947. The economy of western Europe was re-established by their Marshall Plan (1947), which Stalin refused, and the German recovery—its 'economic miracle'—was achieved by 1966. After the Soviet blockade of Berlin (1948–49) the North Atlantic Treaty Organization was set up to include America and Canada as well as Europe. All this served a drive for world power.

Communist countries responded with the Warsaw Pact in 1955, incorporating Hungary in 1956 and Czechoslovakia in 1968, and with the Berlin Wall in 1961, thus forming a buffer zone in East Europe. Half of Europe then cringed under tyranny, the denial of individual freedom, and a tremendous ahrimanic animal will-power lacking human heart forces.

Meanwhile, again under US pressure, decolonization started with Britain leaving India in 1947, and was virtually completed by all European countries by 1961. But the US itself had established military bases all over the 'free' world, dominating its economy and culture.

After difficult negotiations, the European Economic Community fathered by Jean Monnet (1940–55) was formed in 1957 by the Treaty of Rome and centred in Brussels (both Catholic cities), again covering Charlemagne's Holy Roman Empire. This was 33 years after the Christmas Foundation Meeting, and as many years after 1413 as 869 was before it (when the spirit was denied). In the same year the first earth satellite was launched. Britain did not at first join the EEC, but formed a Free Trade Agreement with six others, its application to join in 1961 and 1967 being vetoed by de Gaulle of France. The Community became the European Community, including a political component, in 1967, and expanded to nine countries including Britain in 1972 and to twelve in 1986. The spiritual component was patently lacking, but the Vatican and western Lodges secretively strove to supply it.

The 1960s saw emerge a powerful wave of youthful idealism. But this was perverted by sexual obsession, drug addiction and rock'n'roll music, which together brought a tremendous pollution of the human ego despite the forced crossing of the threshold by individual young people. Many felt subconsciously the Michael-Christ call towards the spirit 33 years after the appearance of the Etheric Christ, the call for new creation, caring for nature, and a real social conscience. But the power of drugs (LSD and marijuana) and of technology undermined their patience and capacity for consciously willed thinking, and they tended to reject western civilization, unable to understand the complex process of its development. The alternative luciferic whimsy of colourful flower-power hippies, however, failed.

To the scientific view of man as an intelligent animal was added the cybernetic view of him as a computer-driven robot. Medicine was increasingly seen in terms of machines and synthetic drugs. Developments such as organ transplants and DNA analysis were offset by the spread of cancer, (and later AIDS) and drug-related illness. Consequently people turned increasingly, where appropriate, to alternative medicine. An impending crisis was gradually recognized, caused by irreparable destruction of the ozone layer, pollution of air and water, wanton destruction of the environment (forests, fish), over-population in the Third World, and an ageing population in the West. But despite much talk, little that was effective was done.

In the 1970s a New Age movement sought to revive ancient lifestyles, with a genuine if over-sentimental concern for the environment—but few were interested in the redemption of thinking or a science of the spirit. There emerged instead the anarchistic, nihilistic punks and skinheads, whose drugs—heroin, cocaine, amphetamines ('speed')—music of frenetic violence, grey-black fashions and acts of self-mutilation were clear marks of ahrimanic inspiration. They rejected both conventional values and the ethos of the previous decade, and were bitterly divided, even tribalized. This was a terribly confused, angry decade, beset by increasing economic decline, fear of nuclear war, fear of unemployment (enhanced by computerization), and a fear of growing crime and terrorism—first glorified on television, then proliferating in reality.

In the 1980s the socialist experiment of the western brotherhoods in Russia was terminated by temporary union with the Polish Pope John Paul II to undermine Soviet control over the eastern bloc (supported by the Solidarity movement of Walensa in Poland) while stepping up the arms race to put formidable pressure on the crumbling

Soviet economy. The enigmatic Gorbachev arose as if from nowhere to cast a spell over the world with his *perestroika* and *glasnost,* as peace was made with Reagan. Much had been learned about totalitarian control of large populations, but the spiritual strength of the Russian people was not destroyed. With the passage of Halley's comet, bringer of materialism, the assault on communism was accompanied by large-scale deregulations of national economies and a new flood of materialistic progress.

The influence of Islam increased steadily throughout the period.

An Opportunity Missed

After 70 years, the Soviet monolith collapsed amid mass emigration, the Berlin Wall fell in 1989, twice 33 years since the Christmas Foundation and about a third of the way through the Michael age. For six months or so idealism flourished again, and there seemed to be a 'window of opportunity'. Europe was no longer divided, its heartland united if not yet healed. Efforts to develop the European Union, stealthily steered mainly by Catholic politicians and bureaucrats and encouraged by America, reached a peak of Euro-optimism.

But in the absence of a true spiritual initiative the opportunity was lost, overwhelmed by the American-led Gulf War and world recession. Western media poured scorn on the possibility of a third way between capitalism and socialism, and the chance to create new forms in the light of Steiner's Threefold Social Ordering was again missed. The dilapidated condition of ex-communist countries placed an enormous strain on newly appointed governments, western aid being made conditional on an immediate switch to a market economy for which the requisite experience simply did not exist. Plans for political union were pushed ahead by western European governments, but where referred to the people with strong government pressure no more than 51% gave their support. High interest rates in Germany due to reunification and substantial help to Russia brought the European economy into depression, with massive unemployment. A criminal Mafia element filled the vacuum, and evidence came to light everywhere, but especially in Italy, of massive fraud and financial manipulation among politicians and business leaders. The morality of the past was clearly failing.

The impulse led by Delors to shape the European Union as a super-state with a single currency continued under Santer, despite widespread hostility outside government circles. The Union was widened to include Austria, Finland and Sweden in 1994, with Poland, Hungary and the Czech Republic being envisaged shortly. France and Germany quietly developed a special relationship with Catholic Poland even before its entry (tripartite ministerial meetings, a joint youth movement, army exercises). The USA progressively disconnected itself from western Europe (troop withdrawals, no soldiers to Bosnia, but supporting NATO), while increasing involvement in Russia (trade, army exercises).

Bolshevism may have had only a short life, but it will be a very long time before humanity will have finished with what stands behind it. If Bolshevik methods prevail, and in succeeding generations they certainly could, then every trace of culture will very soon disappear from the face of the earth. It would mean that the earth would lose its task, would have its mission withdrawn, and would fall a prey to Ahriman. What is to arise in the East in future must develop in opposition to these forces of destruction.[198]

It is some consolation that the development of the spiritual soul requires the forces of evil, so that through overcoming it the individuality may awaken to the spirit, just as it has needed the forces of death which it must transform into spiritual forces. Many individuals are already struggling against the general decline in one way or another. Christianity will not, however, rise from the grave until nationalism and what reaches its peak in Leninism, the luciferic and ahrimanic forms of anti-Christianity respectively, have been overcome.[199]

CONCLUSION

We have seen in European history the interweaving of many spiritual influences. Powerful spiritual beings work through human beings to influence the course of external events in ways which may be benign or harmful, inspired from the future or working on from past ages. Four are of particular significance: those from the south-east and from the north-west; and the adverse powers of Lucifer and Ahriman. From a higher sphere, the love-bearing impulse of Christ stands ready to be called upon by individual human spirits.

Into classical Greece flowed the already ancient impulses of the Persian Mysteries tinged by Lucifer, which were confronted especially by the Greek philosophers. Into the Roman Empire flowed an ahrimanic, mummifying impulse from the Egyptian Mysteries, which was tempered by embalming the personality in Roman law. To this was later added the abstract intellectualism of Gondishapur. The positive impulse of the Grail was virtually suppressed. The outcome was the dogmas of the Church of Rome and the abstract materialism of natural science.

In the north-west lived the cosmic experience of the Hibernian and Northern Mysteries, transmitted through the Arthurian Mysteries to the druidic priesthood. The development of the individuality in Celtic Christianity was rigorously suppressed by Rome but emerged again in weakened form in the Reformation, carried by peasant stock. To this was added the ahrimanic lust for power within the western occult Lodges, linked with the experiment of Bolshevism in the East. The outcome was the egoistic search for material well-being.

There is a real battle in progress between the progressive

and adverse forces. Forces from the progressive Hierarchies only become effective when taken up consciously by the individual through their own spiritual activity, whereas the adverse forces rise instinctively in everyone, but can be fanned to flame in their own interests by the few occultists who are conscious of them. The sphere of production, distribution and consumption of goods needs to be freed from the influence of national economies (particularly that of America) so that world resources can be shared fraternally in the most effective way. Human rights need to be freed from bureaucracy, the laws of ancient Rome, and historical accidents of war and abstract politics, so that people can shape the well-being of a local region to which their feelings can relate. And the creative spheres of education, medicine, science, art and religion need to be freed from political and financial interference, so that the spirituality and skills of each individual can make its fullest contribution to the common good.

Europe has the task of holding the balance between the economic and cultural domination established by America to the west (and its protégé Japan) and the future spirituality of Russia to the east. Within Europe, Central Europe needs to hold the balance between the instinctive development of the consciousness soul in Britain and the preparation of the Slavic peoples for the future descent of the Spirit Self. This depends upon the development in Central Europe, especially in Germany, of understanding for the difference between the selfless quality of the true human 'I' and the pursuit of egoism.

Every people, including the British, have a part to play in the future evolution of Europe, and of the world, but the concept of the nation will have no part in this. The Folk Spirits today need gradually to withdraw (as that of Germany has already done), not to be drawn down into nationalistic disputes—for cosmic impulses that work beyond their due time become tinged with luciferic forces.

Further to what was said on pages 75–76, which remains true, the separate nationalities must today work together towards the soul of Europe as a whole. We must therefore become free from the Folk Soul and turn instead to the all-human within each of us. But the common mission will only exist when people from the different Folk Souls acquire understanding of what one might call 'self-knowledge of the Folk'. This is possible in that whereas every morning the ego descends not only into the body but also into the Folk Soul, every night it plunges into all the Folk Souls other than its own. To feel a relation only to one Folk Soul is thus social egoism. It is necessary to develop love for the neighbouring Folk Spirits. But this may take as long as 1500 years, and the attempt to rush it may only hinder. Theseus needs time to find his way back to Europa.[200]

Into this work the influences of the Planetary Archangels, all of whom are constantly active despite one taking precedence in succession. In each period the previous forces continue to work on with particular strength for about a century, while the new impulse is only gradually finding opportunities to manifest. In the present age of Michael, who took up his task in 1879, that century has passed; and the new impulses seeking a change in culture can now be widely recognized. When one sees that all the sympathy and antipathy poured out today—for instance, in racial hatred—comes only from feelings that are unspiritual and valid only in the physical world, one recognizes the denial of the spirit. Here is one of the deepest secrets of our present culture. It is of the greatest significance for the future evolution of humanity that mankind should be able to take hold of the spirit at the turn of the millennium; out of chaos can arise new creation. But Michael does not in any way compel humanity; only through the adoption by separate individuals of a new level of consciousness can the next step in progressive evolution, on which depend all further steps, be brought to fruition.

In the previous Michael age, people on earth sought to serve Christ as the great Sun Spirit, through reverent observation of sunrise, sunset and the Sun at Midnight. Today Christ has become the Spirit of the Earth, which is to become a sun; and human beings must find again their true nature as sun beings, in order to serve Him for the redemption of the earth. This calls for the extension of the Michaelmas experience of inner sun-glow to that of the cosmic love experienced in the sun-sphere between death and rebirth. But the opposing powers have united to eliminate all knowledge not only of the spirit but also of the soul itself. Only through the spiritual science of Anthroposophy can human beings who individually resist the direction taken by external culture—of whom there are many—find the *conscious* inner path of heart-thinking to the healing forces of Christ.

REFERENCES

Abbreviations: written works of Rudolf Steiner

CMF: *Christianity as Mystical Fact*
CL: *The Course of My Life*
RP: *Riddles of Philosophy*
OS: *Occult Science, an Outline*
T: *Theosophy*
MMT: *Mysticism and Modern Thought*
KHW: *Knowledge of the Higher Worlds/How to Know Higher Worlds*

NB In the following list of references, [?] indicates that I cannot relocate the source of the quotation from Rudolf Steiner.

Introduction

1. 30.8.22, 1.7.24, 17.10.20, 18.10.18.
2. 17.3.23, 23.9.16.
3. John Meeks, *The Golden Blade*, 1979.
4. 2.5.13, 19.1.15.
5. 15.4.09, 22.3.10. Douglas Caughill, *Anthroposophy Today*, 23, 1994.
6. 14.11.14.
7. Robert Graves, *The Greek Myths* (Penguin Books, 1955).
8. 12.6.10a, 8.8.20, 20.6.16.
9. 8.6.10, 9.6.10.
10. 13.9.14, 31.10.14.
11. Guenther Wachsmuth, *The Life and Work of Rudolf Steiner* (New York: Whittier Books, 1955).
12. 14.11.14.
13. 26.12.23, 25.5.21.

Chapter 1

14. 27.9.23, 5.10.23, 8.8.24, 13.10.23, 19.7.24, 2.5.13.
15. 17.11.23a, 12.4.09, 1.4.13, 29.11.07, T, 25.7.20, 22.1.14.
16. 24.4.22, 7.7.24, 23.3.11, 13.8.24, 21.8.24b, 16.8.24.
17. T, CMF, 30.8.09, 30.12.13.
18. 2.12.23, 18.8.11, 19.8.11, CMF.
19. 29.12.23.
20. 29.4.21, 11.5.21, 3.6.21, CMF, 8.8.24, 1.5.21, 17.4.21.
21. 24.12.23, 5.5.10, 29.4.21, 27.12.11.
22. 5.6.21, 29.12.23,[?].
23. [?], 17.9.16, 31.12.23.
24. RP.
25. RP, 3.4.17, 22.1.14, 10.1.15.
26. 16.4.21, 4.3.23, 5.6.21.
27. RP, 25.12.23, 16.4.21.
28. 18.10.04, 12.6.10b, 18.10.04, 30.7.18, 24.4.17.

Chapter 2

29. 8.8.24, 12.10.23.
30. OS, 3.11.12, 2.9.23, 22.4.24, 16.8.24.
31. 22.3.11, 29.11.07, 16.11.22, 1.7.22.
32. 27.7.23, 17.11.23b, 2.9.23.
33. 13.11.23, 24.12.23, 11.6.12, 12.11.22.
34. 1.4.13, T, 1.7.22, 22.1.14, 1.4.13, 16.8.24.
35. 18.10.04, 10.1.15, 16.9.16.
36. 16.5.21. 16.9.16, 5.6.21.
37. 18.10.04, 12.6.10b.
38. 17.9.16, 18.10.04.
39. 16.4.21, 16.6.10, 7.10.16.
40. 3.11.18, 15.11.14.
41. 12.6.10b, 15.3.24. Guenther Wachsmuth, *The Evolution of Mankind* (Dornach: CH 1961).
42. 13.10.18, 14.4.17.
43. 3.4.17.
44. 22.1.14, 1.5.21, 9.4.21, 27.3.17, 20.5.08.
45. 27.3.17, 17.4.17.
46. 20.2.20.
47. 10.4.17, 27.3.17, 16.5.21, 13.6.20, 24.4.17.
48. [?], 16.9.16.

Chapter 3

49. 22.4.24, 17.11.23a, 29.11.07, 7.7.24, 1.4.13, T, 12.4.09, 18.5.13.
50. 16.8.24, 22.3.10, 1.4.13, 22.1.14.
51. 12.11.22, 30.6.22, 23.3.11, 13.8.24.
52. 8.7.24.
53. 16.10.18, 31.8.23.
54. 15.4.21, 23.5.21, RP.
55. 3.11.18, 19.7.04, 19.9.24.
56. 17.4.17, 23.5.21, 17.4.17.
57. 12.6.10b, 16.5.21.
58. 19.4.17, 10.1.15, 17.9.16.
59. 7.12.23, 9.12.23, 27.8.24, 1.10.22.
60. 16.3.23, 28.7.24, 10.1.15, 23.9.22, 29.11.19.
61. 15.5.21, 16.5.21, 31.8.09.
62. 15.6.10, 24.7.15, 18.10.04, 3.11.18.
63. 16.5.21, 14.6.10, 15.11.14, 25.10.04, 16.5.21.
64. [?], 15.5.21.
65. 24.7.15, 18.12.16, 18.10.04, 1.10.13.
66. 26.10.07, 24.7.15.
67. 16.5.21, 25.12.23, 22.1.17.
68. 24.7.15, 21.12.16, 26.10.07, 22.1.17.
69. 26.10.07, 22.1.17, 25.10.04, 3.11.18, 24.7.15.
70. 4.12.21, 1.11.04.
71. 16.7.18.
72. 9.12.23, 19.1.15, 22.1.17.
73. 30.7.18, 24.7.15.

Chapter 4

74. 17.11.23b, 3.11.12, 12.4.09, 22.4.24.
75. 27.7.23, 16.11.22, 27.7.23.
76. 16.11.22, 12.6.10a, 13.8.24, 22.1.14, 30.6.22.
77. 1.4.13, T, 7.7.24.
78. 23.3.11, 1.7.22, 16.8.24, 12.6.10a.
79. 7.12.23, 9.12.23.
80. 7.2.13.
81. 4.1.24, [?], 2.6.21.
82. 11.7.24.
83. 16.10.18, 12.10.18, 29.6.08.
84. 13.3.11, 16.8.08.

85. 8.11.04, 1.7.24, 13.3.11,[?].
86. 16.4.21, 3.6.21.
87. 6.12.04, 25.10.04, 3.12.05, 1.11.04.
88. 6.5.09, 3.11.18.
89. [?], 23.11.18, 16.6.10.

Chapter 5

90. 7.10.23, 13.10.23.
91. 27.7.23, 22.3.10, 15.8.24, 21.8.24a, 17.11.23a, 1.4.13, T.
92. 7.7.24, 1.7.22, 11.6.12, 22.1.14, 23.12.23, 6.1.08.
93. 11.6.12, 23.3.11, 22.4.24, 16.8.24, 30.6.22, 18.8.24.
94. 27.8.24, 21.8.24, 7.2.13.
95. 1.10.22, 11.7.24.
96. 16.5.21, 13.12.04, 13.10.18, 3.11.18.
97. 10.1.15, 16.10.18, 12.10.18.
98. 8.8.24, [?], 13.12,04, 16.5.21.
99. Sergei Prokofieff, *The Spiritual Origins of Eastern Europe and the Future Mysteries of the Holy Grail* (Temple Lodge, 1993). 9.11.14, 2.11.18.
100. 28.3.16, 21.2.15.
101. 7.3.14, 7.2.13, 13.7.24, 6.12,04, 14.8.24.
102. 18.10.18, 16.5.21.
103. 18.10.04, 16.5.21, 23.5.21, 24.5.21, 8.11.04, 27.3.17.
104. 1.9.10, 17.3.23, 20.12.04, 15.4.21, 19.10.18.
105. 25.9.16, 20.12.04, 18.8.24.

Chapter 6

106. 1.1.12, 1.4.13.
107. 25.6.08, 7.7.24, 27.7.23, 23.3.11, 22.1.14, 30.6.22.
108. 27.7.23, 12.4.09, 22.4.24, 17.11.23b, T.
109. 1.4.13, T, 13.8.24, KHW, 22.12.12.
110. 13.7.24, 18.12.12, 18.10.18.
111. 30.10.20, 2.6.21.
112. 5.1.24, 4.1.24.
113a. 18.10.18, 12.6.10a, 17.9.16, 24.9.16. Karl Heyer, *The Middle Ages* (Forest Row: Steiner Schools Fellowship Publications, 1994).
113b. 23.11.18. Sergei Prokofieff, *The Spiritual Origins of Eastern*

Europe and the Future Mysteries of the Holy Grail (Temple Lodge, 1993).
114. 18.11.17.
115. 9.2.12.
116. 1.7.24, RP, 23.5.21, 14.1.15, MMT, 5.1.24.
117. 12.10.18.
118. 18.10.18, 25.9.16, 19.10.18.
119. 28.7.24, 28.10.17.
120. T, 12.6.10b, 28.7.24, 20.7.24, 30.3.19.
121. 2.6.21, 16.5.21, RP, 29.4.21.
122. 18.10.04, 16.5.21.
123. 17.1.15, 18.10.18, 28.3.16.
124. 16.5.21, 11.4.16.
125. 31.12.23, 6.1.24.
126. 7.1.24, 10.10.15, 23.10.15.
127. 20.10.18, 25.11.18, 16.7.18.
128. 28.10.17, 17.9.16.
129. 22.12.12, 18.12.12.

Chapter 7

130. 13.10.23, 1.6.13.
131. 12.4.09, 2.9.23, 30.5.24, 20.5.08, 14.4.12.
132. T, 1.7.22, 7.7.24, 22.3.10, 6.1.08.
133. 25.8.10, 29.11.07, 17.11.23b, 11.6.12, 16.8.14.
134. 22.1.14.
135. RP, 17.3.23, 18.9.17, 20.12.04, 2.11.18, 28.7.24.
136. 16.12.16, 17.12.16.
137. 2.11.18, 23.10.20, 29.4.21, 9.5.16.
138. 31.10.14.
139. 18.10.18, 28.7.24.
140. 3.12.14.
141. 14.1.15, 28.11.14, [?].
142. 17.9.16.
143. 16.3.15, 28.1.17, 8.6.10.
144. 31.10.14.
145. 30.4.21, 9.2.16, 10.10.05, 20.10.18.
146. 19.10.18.
147. 30.4.21, 1.5.21.
148. 18.10.18, 23.4.22, 10.1.16.

149. 19.10.18, 16.11.18, 4.4.16, 19.10.18, 28.3.16.
150. 23.10.20, 16.3.15, 9.12.16, 20.2.20.
151. 24.7.15, 17.3.23.
152. 1.5.21, RP.
153. 22.10.20, 12.12.18, 30.4.21, 3.11.18.
154. 15.11.04, 9.12.23.
155. 18.10.18, 25.9.17.
156. 9.6.10, 10.10.14, RP.
157. 31.10.14.
158. RP, 30.4.21.
159. 16.3.15, 30.10.20. Sergei Prokofieff, *The Spiritual Origins of Eastern Europe and the Future Mysteries of the Holy Grail* (Temple Lodge, 1993).
160. Ibid., 3.11.18.
161. Ibid.
162. 9.12.16, 28.3.16, 9.1.21, 23.8.20, 4.4.16, 1.5.21.
163. 28.1.17.
164. [?], 6.7.24, 17.2.18, 14.10.17.
165. 7.12.18.
166. 28.10.17, 1.5.21, 24.4.21, 15.5.21, 7.10.16.
167. 2.5.13, 30.7.18, 30.5.20, 22.1.17.
168. 20.10.18, 23.10.20, 3.11.18, 16.5.21.
169. 24.5.21, 20.10.18.
170. 29.4.21, 19.10.18, 25.10.18.
171. 20.10.18, 3.11.18, 15.5.21, 27.3.17, 25.10.18.
172. 10.10.15, 17.10.15, 1.5.21.
173. 6.7.15, 20.10.18.
174. 30.4.21.
175. 12.4.19.
176. 20.10.18.

Chapter 8

177. 8.8.24, 13.10.23, 2.5.13, 12.6.10b.
178. 2.5.13, 28.7.24, 8.8.24, 12.6.10b, 20.7.21.
179. 12.6.10b, 16.3.15, 6.7.24.
180. 17.12.18, 6.7.24, 19.1.15, 8.8.24.
181. 1.8.24, 23.11.19, 30.11.19, 21.8.24b, 18.8.24.
182. 22.11.19, 19.7.24, 8.8.24, 27.9.23.
183. 2.11.18, 7.10.16, 30.4.21.

184. 11.10.15.
185. CL.
186. 3.11.12, 3.6.21, 13.5.21.
187. Sergei Prokofieff, *Rudolf Steiner and the Founding of the New Mysteries*, 2nd ed. (Temple Lodge, 1994). 6.2.17.
188. 4.12.16, 1.12.18, 12.12.18, 17.12.18.
189. 11.12.16, 22.12.18.
190. 18.12.16, 3.6.21, [?].
191. 11.12.16.
192. 25.10.18, 24.11.18, 16.11.17, 17.4.21.
193. 26.10.18, 6.2.20.
194. 31.8.23.
195. 25.1.10, 8.8.24, 21.9.11.
196. 29.6.08. 20.9.24.
197. Sergei Prokofieff, *The Spiritual Origins of Eastern Europe* (Temple Lodge, 1993).
198. 6.5.20, 3.6.20, 25.8.19, 22.8.19, 7.8.20.
199. 25.10.18, 3.4.20.

Conclusion

200. 25.10.18, 25.8.11.

BIBLIOGRAPHY

Note: Only lectures contained in volumes published in English are shown here. (For publication lists contact Rudolf Steiner Press, London, or Anthroposophic Press, New York.) For all others—in news-sheets, in typescript, untranslated or unpublished—please consult a major anthroposophical library. The numbers before the title refer to the collected German edition (*Gesamtausgabe*).

10.10.05	93a	*Foundations of Esotericism*
6.1.08	102	*The Influence of Spiritual Beings upon Man*
20.5.08	103	*The Gospel of St. John* (Hamburg)
25.6.08 and 29.6.08	104	*The Apocalypse of St. John*
16.8.08	106	*Universe, Earth and Man*
12.4.09 and 15.4.09	110	*The Spiritual Hierarchies*
30.8.09 and 31.8.09	113	*The East in the Light of the West*
25.1.10	118	*The True Nature of the Second Coming*
22.3.10	119	*Macrocosm and Microcosm*
5.5.10	59	*Metamorphoses of the Soul*, Vol. 1
8.6.10 to 16.6.10	121	*The Mission of the Individual Folk Souls in Relation to Teutonic Mythology*
25.8.10	122	*Genesis: Secrets of the Bible Story of Creation*
1.9.10	123	*The Gospel of St. Matthew*
13.3.11	124	*Background to the Gospel of St. Mark*
22.3.11 and 23.3.11	128	*Occult Physiology*
18.8.11 to 25.8.11	129	*Wonders of the World*
21.9.11	130	*From Buddha to Christ*
27.12.11	134	*The World of the Senses and the World of the Spirit*
9.2.12 and 18.12.12	130	*Esoteric Christianity and the Mission of Christian Rosenkreutz*

13.4.12 and 14.4.12	136	*The Spiritual Beings in the Heavenly Bodies and in the Kingdoms of Nature*
11.6.12	137	*Man in the Light of Occultism, Theosophy and Philosophy*
3.11.12	140	*Life Between Death and Rebirth*
22.12.12 and 1.4.13	141	*Between Death and Rebirth*
7.2.13	144	*The Mysteries of the East and of Christianity*
2.5.13	152	*Occult Science and Occult Development*
1.6.13	146	*The Occult Significance of the Bhagavad Gita*
1.10.13	148	*The Fifth Gospel*
30.12.13	149	*Christ and the Spiritual World and the Search for the Holy Grail*
22.1.14	151	*Human and Cosmic Thought*
31.10.14 to 6.7.15*	157	*Destinies of Individuals and of Nations*
9.11.14 to 15.11.14	158	*The Spiritual Hierarchies*
10.10.15 to 23.10.15	254	*Occult Movements in 19th Century*
16.9.16 to 25.9.16	171	*Inner Impulses of Human Evolution*
4.12.16 to 21.12.16	173	*The Karma of Untruthfulness*, Vol. 1
22.1.17 and 28.1.17	174	*The Karma of Untruthfulness*, Vol. 2
6.2.17	175	*Cosmic and Human Metamorphoses*
27.3.17 to 24.4.17	175	*Building Stones for an Understanding of the Mystery of Golgotha*
18.9.17 and 25.9.17	176	*The Karma of Materialism*
14.10.17 and 28.10.17	177	*The Fall of the Spirits of Darkness*
18.11.17	178	*The Wrong and Right Use of Esoteric Knowledge*
17.2.18	174a	*The Mission of the Archangel Michael*
12.10.18 and 13.10.18	184	*Three Streams in Human Evolution*
18.10.18 to 3.11.18	185	*From Symptom to Reality in Modern History*
1.12.18 and 7.12.18	186	*The Challenge of the Times*
22.12.18	187	*The Birth of Christ in the Human Soul*
22.8.19 and 25.8.19	293	*Study of Man*
22.11.19 to 30.11.19	194	*The Mission of the Archangel Michael*
20.2.20	196	*Ideas for a New Europe*
3.4.20	198	*The Festivals and their Meaning, II Easter*

25.7.20	197	*Polarities in the Evolution of Mankind*
22.10.20 to 30.10.20	200	*The New Spirituality and the Christ Experience of the Twentieth Century*
9.4.21 to 20.7.21*	204	*Materialism and the Task of Anthroposophy*
23.5.21 and 24.5.21	325	*Natural Science and Evolution*
4.12.21	209	*Cosmic Forces in Man*
20.4.22 to 16.11.22*	211 (plus others)	*Planetary Spheres and Their Influence on Man's Life on Earth and in the Spiritual Worlds*
30.6.22 and 1.7.22	213	*Human Questions and Cosmic Answers*
23.9.22 and 1.10.22	216	*Supersensible Influences in the History of Mankind*
16.3.23 and 17.3.23	222	*The Driving Force of Spiritual Powers in World History*
31.8.23	227	*The Evolution of Consciousness*
2.9.23	228	*Man as a Picture of the Living Spirit*
27.9.23	223	*Michaelmas and the Soul Forces of Man*
5.10.23 to 13.10.23	229	*Four Seasons and the Archangels*
13.11.23 and 17.11.23	231	*Supersensible Man*
2.12.23 to 23.12.23	232	*Mystery Knowledge and Mystery Centres*
24.12.23 to 31.12.23	233	*World History in the Light of Anthroposophy*
4.1.24 to 7.1.24	233a	*Rosicrucianism and Modern Initiation*
22.4.24	233a	*The Easter Festival*
30.5.24	236	*Karmic Relationships*, Vol. II
1.7.24 to 8.8.24*	237	*Karmic Relationships*, Vol. III
19.7.24 and 20.7.24	240	*Karmic Relationships*, Vol. VI
7.7.24	279	*Eurythmy as Visible Speech*
13.8.24 to 21.8.24	243	*True and False Paths in Spiritual Investigation*
21.8.24 to 19.9.24	240	*Karmic Relationships*, Vol. VIII

* Other lectures between these dates are not in this volume.

THE END OF THE MILLENNIUM
and beyond

from the work of
RUDOLF STEINER

compiled and edited by
RICHARD SEDDON

'The forces that have so far guided human progress will be exhausted by the middle of this century', declared Rudolf Steiner in 1919. Elsewhere he spoke of 'an acute illness of civilisation', or 'a real blind alley which will end in catastrophe—the beginning of the Earth's death'. Richard Seddon has gathered together many of the comments Steiner made regarding the end of the millennium and beyond, creating a mosaic of his indications on this subject. The bibliography enables the reader to study Steiner's often dramatic words in their full context and depth.

64pp; 21.5 x 13.5 cm; paperback; ISBN 0 904693 46 5

TEMPLE LODGE PUBLISHING